COACH
CULTURE

COACH CULTURE

A PLAYBOOK FOR
WINNING IN BUSINESS

Black Butte Publishing

First Printing, 2017

Black Butte Publishing
createnonfiction.com

ACKNOWLEDGMENTS

Many people were instrumental in helping me produce this book. I am truly grateful for the following:

For spending time with me and sharing about their successful coaching programs within their businesses; Matt Becker, Christine Barnes, Dawn Pons, Doug Flor, Stefan Wiedner, Tess Richardson, Michael Nunemaker.

For invaluable feedback on the first draft of the book, especially Ed Nottingham, Carl Dierschow, and Chris Sier, thank you for steering the ship.

For the many who contributed quotes and citations, as well as the research used: Human Capital Institute, the International Coach Federation, The Gallup Organization, Michael Bungay Stanier, Michael D. Watkins, Stephen R Covey, Lisa Ann Edwards, Patricia Pulliam Phillips, Jack J Phillips, Sir John Whitmore, Judith Glaser, Michael J Marquardt, Tony Stoltzfus, Merianne Liteman, Sheila Campbell, Jeff Liteman, Lisa Haneberg, Jack Canfield, Brian O Underhill, Mel Robbins, Dan Pink, L Robert Kohls, William Bridges, Peter Drucker, Steve Chandler, Dave Packard, Jack Welch, Jerome Abarbanel, Fortune Magazine, Carl Dierschow, Ed Nottingham, Stephan Wiedner, Ray Smith, Business Wire,

Regina Leeds, Jeannine Jacobsen, Zappos, Laura Berman
Fortgang, Janice Flor, Alastair Robertson, Medallia.com,
Don Kirkpatrick, Coach U, Danny Dalrymple, Marshall
Goldsmith, Beyond Emancipation, GlaxoSmithKline,
Blessingwhite, Tech CU, Alister Scott and Neil Scotton,
William Oncken Jr and Donald L Wass, Brad Herbert
and Sonia Strobel, Isikkent Schools and the ICF Internal
Coaching community of practice.

For my colleagues who helped me form our global internal coaching and training programs to support talent
management efforts, that ultimately helped form chap-
ters in this book: John Hardwick, Ray Mera, Brett Walk-
er, and Steve Woolston.

For encouragement, guidance and mentoring throughout
my coaching career, as well as this book Cassi Christian-
sen and Pamela Richarde. Yay!

For always believing I had a book in me: Diana Cauley
and Ann Craig.

For Mark Ruth and Abby Heverin at the ICF, your research and work with the ICF International Prism award
and inspiring its winners provided ample examples of the
breadth and depth of coaching application and its results.
I am also grateful to the many coaches who have sub-
mitted their coaching stories as applicants for the Prism
award, especially those cited in the book. Your striving
and results have lifted the profession.

For Jim DuPree, who took a big risk, and won even bigger, creating a legacy with our internal programs. I am forever grateful for your faith in me.

For my editor Esbe van Heerden and the team at Non-Fiction, your guidance and wisdom made the whole process rewarding and enjoyable.

Finally, for John, Cassandra and Sophie, you are precious—you have endured me with my unsolicited coach hat on more times than I can count, and your unwavering support from day one of this coaching journey through this endeavor was my rock. You are my favorites.

CONTENTS

INTRODUCTION

The knots in your stomach tighten like a python, you've run through—and stressed out about—each one of your deadlines already, and you haven't even finished making your morning coffee. Cortisol floods through your body on your commute as you anticipate each reaction and challenge you might face today. You cringe upon entering the building, and again at the thought of what might be facing you in your ever-shrinking cubicle, in your ever-growing inbox, and at today's ever-boring meetings.

You've been showing up to the office earlier and earlier, to grab a moment of peace—no matter how tiny—to prepare for the day, but everyone else is doing it too, and so all you've achieved is a routine of working longer hours. Today, just like yesterday, and the day before that, your authority, your leadership and your territory will be challenged.

You must monitor your staff's actions, positioning and even presentations, to be sure that you look like you know what you are doing at all times. You can't even trust them to make sound judgments in their projects. You have to oversee everything and insert your experience at every turn. How much longer can you keep this up? You can't say anything to your boss, what if she thinks you are incompetent if you ask for help? Can you risk looking bad? If you don't make your numbers this quarter, one of the managers will be gone—and it can't be you. You've got a kid going to college next year, and another in two more years. It won't be long before your mom's cute forgetfulness becomes a memory care problem.

You feel as if the only option is to keep your head down and put in the hours—all of the hours. They can't let you go if you keep meeting your objectives, right? It's such a high cost to pay.

What if I told you there was another way? That instead of your morning and your life looking like that, it could sound like this:

The alarm goes off in the bathroom, after reading Mel Robbins' *The 5-Second Rule*, you decided to implement that change so you recite to yourself "5-4-3-2-1-Go!" And you're out of bed. It's going to be an excellent day.

Today is quarterly business reviews. And you can't wait. You'll get to see all the progress your team has achieved with very little effort or time invested on your part, because you changed your leadership style, and implemented a coaching culture six months ago. Instead of your team members depending on you for not only what to do, but how to do it, they use you for guidance, check-ins, and air cover. They are more engaged, are taking more ownership and are excited to co-create results with their peers at work.

Innovation is at an all-time high because risk-taking is truly encouraged and what was once a no-fail zone allows for learning and growth. You've come a long way from the extended hours, controlling behavior and dealing with the bullying and sabotage amongst your staff and your own peers that was happening out of fear, uncertainty, and doubt. Instead of always judging and shooting down the ideas of others for personal gain, your team has become curious and trusting. Implementing this coaching approach has improved your day-to-day work experience, the employees' engagement levels, the company's financial performance, and it has transformed the relationships with your family and community as well.

So, what should you do about it? How do you get to a place of enjoyment as a leader, and increase the engagement of your employees?

The answer, quite simply, is a coach culture.

According to Gallup, 87% of employees worldwide are not engaged at work. Companies with highly engaged workforces outperform their peers by 147% in earnings per share.

The research conducted by the Human Capital Institute (HCI) and the International Coach Federation (ICF) shows that companies with a strong coaching culture, outperform their peers financially and enjoy higher rates of highly engaged employees.

2013 revenue growth in relation to industry peer group by coaching culture.

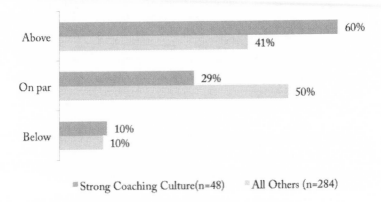

■ Strong Coaching Culture(n=48)   ▪ All Others (n=284)

Highly engaged employees by coaching culture.

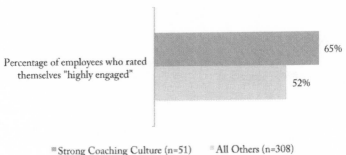

■ Strong Coaching Culture (n=51)   ▪ All Others (n=308)

So, with that information, why don't more companies build a coaching culture? The top three factors cited for not implementing a coaching culture are:

- a lack of time
- inability to measure return on investment (ROI)
- funding

In this book, we'll cover *The What, The Why, The Options* and *The How* of building a coaching culture. We'll demonstrate that creating a coaching culture will save you and your leaders time, increase your employee engagement (productivity, profitability, and employee retention) and that the savings from these results alone will fund the coaching program. And for those of you who want more proof? We'll review an alternative to measuring ROI, with return on expectation (ROE).

TURNOVER

The turnover problem was especially fierce, and it was easy to see why. The average Joe's day was not fun. First, he gets up with dread. He knows he's going to work, where one of two things will happen: either he'll enter into an ongoing battle to have his ideas heard—which is exhausting—or he will give up. He's not even going to submit his ideas anymore. He's checked out, but he's still collecting his paycheck. Joe's problem is not isolated to him. Collectively, this looks like a high turnover rate. With one such company, their turnover was at 13%, until they implemented a coaching culture.

With a coaching culture, ideas are heard, curiosity and exploring are encouraged. Teams move from "I" to "We." When employees start checking out, or productivity slips, instead of avoiding it, leaders step in and ask how things are going—is everything ok at home? What can I do to encourage your innovation?

When the leaders at Joe's company experienced coaching for themselves, they saw the benefits and made the determination to expand the program to every employee. The whole organization was trained in coaching

skills. With their newfound coaching skills, they started asking open-ended questions, they began actively listening, paraphrasing for understanding, and finally they
were engaging instead of arguing. Program development
became a coaching session, a team-focused collaboration.

Can you guess what happened to turnover?

Instead of allowing an environment where the loudest voice always wins, they used a coaching approach. This
created a shift across the company. People started bonding
as they worked, and their turnover was reduced by *over a
third*. That kind of reduced turnover can save a company
millions in training alone. Their corporate culture went
from a hostile environment with a high turnover (and a
weak product) to the golden girl of their industry. Everyone wanted to work there!

ENGAGEMENT

By building a coaching culture at my own company, we
increased employee engagement by four hundred percent,
validated through our own internal surveys with an established baseline.

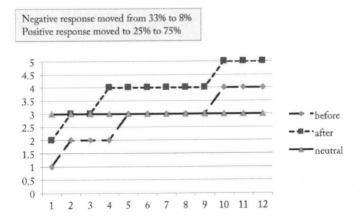

It wasn't a small project, I was one coach in a department of ten thousand people, but the size didn't matter. Size is often the factor that deters companies the fastest—you think a coaching program *has* to be one-on-one, but that's not the case. Sometimes, it's even easier in big groups.

Think about it this way: What makes an engaged employee?

Gallup introduced the Q12 survey many years ago, which asks employees twelve key questions across these four categories:

1.) What do I give?

2.) What do I get?

3.) Do I belong?

4.) Do I have an opportunity to grow?

Gallup's science is based on 30 years of research with more than 30 million employees. Are you wondering what the value of an engaged employee is? A strong correlation between both productivity and retention sits with the engaged employee, which translates to less recruiting, hiring, and onboarding of employees, and once they are established, they are more productive than their peers. That productivity and retention turns into profitability.

Many companies have their own similar surveys to define how engaged their employees are; my company's was called the Voice of the Workforce survey, and it was measured annually. The most important question on that survey, in my mind, was paraphrased like this:

"Do you actually think management is going to do anything with this data?"

When employees answer no to that question, it's as if they've already given up. They feel unmotivated, unheard, unimportant. They don't believe the survey matters. My job included creating the corrective action plan for this survey, and that was the question I most wanted to impact. If an employee feels like management is going to listen to them, they feel valued at that company. I might not have had control over corporate headquarters; I couldn't give anyone a raise, or more vacation time, or better benefits. But you know what?

That's not what motivates people.

MOTIVATION

One of my best friends and I called one of my previous workplaces "The Borg." We joked with each other about whether we'd be "assimilated." (If you're unfamiliar with this Star Trek reference, all you probably need to know is that The Borg are an alien race and that their first human encounter with the Star Trek crew begins with "You will be assimilated, resistance is futile"). Obviously, we didn't feel very connected to that greater company culture—but we had each other. We knew there was at least one other person who felt the same as us, and we could keep coming to work. We unintentionally created our own mini-coaching culture, which kept us motivated when the company didn't. Many of the same attributes that create a formal, intentional coaching culture—trust, listening, support, strategizing, and accountability—were present in that friendship. Imagine how much more motivated we would have been if that culture was company-wide?

In the book, *Drive: The Surprising Truth About What Motivates Us*, author Dan Pink cites a study which found that once people are paid adequately—defined by Pink as 'pay people enough to take the issue of money off of the table'—money no longer motivates them. What motivates them is autonomy, mastery, and purpose.

Autonomy: Employees want to set their own direction. Instead of a manager directing them on how to do it, they should be free to come up with their own solutions.

Mastery: Employees should have the freedom to grow and develop in their skillset. They create their own development plan (autonomy) and receive support to improve themselves.

Purpose: Employees need to feel connected to what they do, to have a why, to feel like what they're doing matters and to believe in the mission and values of the company—and their role within it. Illustrating the connection of an employee's performance objectives to department business plans and/or company goals helps demonstrate purpose as well.

These are cultural things—they're all about the culture of the company. Without these three things, there's no room for questions, no room for growth, no room to simply say, "I need help."

These are also key aspects of coaching.

OVERWORKED AND DISCONNECTED

All of us, unfortunately, are probably familiar with the corporate culture of layoffs. As companies struggled through the recession, they chose to cut headcounts rather than cut their scope of work. That created a kind of survivor syndrome: employees feel guilty that their co-workers were laid off, but they're also thinking, 'Thank God it wasn't me.' They put their heads down, hoping that if they work hard enough, they won't be next. The reality is, even today, everyone is replaceable. No matter how many hours you work, there are no guarantees.

I had a client once who was assigned to me after he'd had a heart attack. He was a Type-A salesperson and worked upwards of 80 hours every week. Unsurprisingly, his health suffered. He had a heart attack and was forced to take time off. Eventually, he was completely laid off. But that wasn't the worst part. After he was laid off, his attitude towards his family was eager—he was excited to have more time with them, to participate with them, to connect with them.

But they couldn't connect with him. They had their own activities, their own lives, and he hadn't been around for any of it up until then. What he had seen as a loving action—serving and providing for his family—felt to them like abandonment. He never had time for them; they never felt loved by him. Here he was, ready to be with his family after almost dying, and they could barely give him the time of day because they still felt unloved.

That's the kind of tragedy I see every day; that's the kind of tragedy born from unhealthy work environments. Even for those that remain at work, it's not much better. Stress-induced illnesses like migraines, stomach aches, and ulcers, abound. People are working horrific hours in the hopes of saving their job, constantly on the alert, looking over their shoulder, terrified. They want to be noticed, yet invisible—they want to remain, yet there's no peace in remaining.

So how does this get improved with a coaching culture? With coaching competencies like building trust and being present, both the leader and the employee have the opportunity to engage in dialogue that creates awareness about the building tension and fear. Further competencies like effective communication ensure that there is a great understanding between parties, Judith E. Glaser Chairman, The CreatingWe Institute and Co-Founder C-IQ for Coaches and the author of *Conversational Intelligence*, uses a term "double-clicking." Just like we would on a web page link to learn more, we learn to double-click on phrases like overwork, work-life balance, and what being noticed means. And finally, the competencies of facilitating learning and results-dialogue creates awareness, which allows actions to be designed to meet goals, and everyone manages the progress and accountability.

EXPERTS ONLY

Often, companies have a "four-quadrant system" to manage talent. The first quadrant, "new to the job," means they want to develop you. You haven't quite mastered the job that you're in yet, so you've got lots of room for growth. The next quadrant is "not making the cut," which implies you're in the wrong job, or perhaps the job is beyond your skillset. Then there's "high potential," which means you might not have mastered the job, but you have an eagerness and willingness to learn or make a big move. You're committed, and you have potential. Finally, there's "expert," which is just what it sounds like. You've mastered the job, and the only thing left for you is to pursue new developments in whatever field you need to grow.

The problem is that (thanks to this culture of layoffs) everyone wants to stay in the expert category. It makes sense; it's certainly the safest place to be. But a lot of the "high-potential" opportunities are missed. There's too much risk in that quadrant; it might require, for example, a move to a new city. Does anyone want to uproot their family, take their children out of school, maybe place their parents in an eldercare system, just to go off somewhere and possibly fail in this new challenge? If I know the company is not going to have my back, why would I take that risk? No—better to fight to stay in the "experts" quadrant.

Unfortunately, this experts-only mentality can breed contempt. It makes for employees who are not only unexcited about coming to work, but they're bringing down the community around them. It's a fear-based environment where people are afraid to ask questions or even for clarification. They want to keep their head down. Once, one of the VP's of a company I worked with casually asked an engineer for information. *Very* casually, as in, "Gosh, I wonder how much that costs? How many of our customers have that?" It was a think-out-loud, pondering type of question, not a heavy, top-priority question.

But the poor engineer who heard him didn't know that and didn't feel comfortable asking to clarify. This was a Friday at 3:00 PM or so, and the engineer had no choice but to take this request as gospel. He couldn't question, he couldn't push back, so he went all in. He spent forty-two hours that weekend running reports and researching. Then, when he delivered all the info to the VP, the response was, "Oh, cool." It was almost inconsequential.

That engineer never asked what the priority was. He never asked if spending an extra weekend and a couple thousand dollars to come up with that information was essential; he just did it. And how do you think he felt afterward?

Certainly not motivated or connected.

FEAR: A LESSON FROM VOLKSWAGEN

A fear-based environment does more than just wear down employees. 'In September of 2015, VW- A German Automaker, "admitted they installed on-board computer software designed to cheat on government emissions test in nearly 500,000 of its four-cylinder 'clean diesel cars' sold in the U.S." *(Associated Press and Reuters)*. The top executive in the U.S. told lawmakers that this was not a corporate decision but actions taken by software engineers.

Whether that statement is wholly accurate or not, is irrelevant, what is relevant is that VW had created a culture that compelled employees to create a workaround to meet performance objectives. A culture created by an executive's directive to achieve goals. As of April 2017, VW was expecting the first rulings in the legal cases resulting from the scandal. After the initial admission in September of 2015, the lawsuits expanded to four, with 47 people indicted with some duplicates. The number of cars affected by this scandal included 11 million.

How did that happen?

Often, when something like this happens—and it frequently happens with less widespread and visible results—it isn't just the accident of one person. It's part of a team effort with multiple contributors. Some executive order must have come down, some decree demanding, "Make it happen." In a fear-based culture, people are so desperate to keep their jobs that they'll comply. It's a rationalization process: If we don't get our efficiency to forty miles a gallon, then thirty people in our department are going to get laid off." Or maybe, "If I don't do it, somebody else will—and then I'll get the ax and they won't."

"What's your version of this story?"

THE HEADLINE TEST

In 2016, Neil Scotton, PCC, International Coach Federation, Co-Founder of the One Leadership Project and Dr. Alister Scott published an article 'Three Minutes to Midnight: What's the Point of Coaching' and refer to " 'cultures of fear'; places where 'if you care about your future, you don't tell the boss the real story.' There were examples of careers damaged by whistleblowing... A simple truth emerged that if a leader makes us 'feel on edge,' chances are others feel it too, and the truth will not be spoken to them. And that has big consequences."

In a coaching culture, the organization would feel free to ask "How would this headline read?" Perhaps there is another way...

A NEED FOR CONTROL

The rationalizations don't stop at employees. Managers have to rationalize their behavior, too. It can sound like "For my department to perform, I need to control how my employees do things, or what they say or who they interact with, and I can't possibly allow for additional innovation that may not produce great results." They're feeling the pressure, too. Not only do they have to be first among equals—they feel pressure to be the best on their team, or their job's at risk—they also have projects that they have to run. This contributes to a need to control; a death grip on every employee. There isn't room for innovation. In most Fortune 50 consumer companies, when new ideas are proposed, if such new ideas cannot achieve a billion-dollar market, it is often discarded. Investments in R&D and other resources require great discretion, and there is no room for minor innovations.

THE CHALLENGE OF DELEGATION

An article that was originally published in the Nov-Dec 1974 Harvard Business Review (HBR), and reprinted in 1999, that has been one of the publication's two best-selling reprints ever—"Management Time: Who's Got the Monkey?" by William Oncken Jr. and Donald L. Wass, discusses the challenge of delegation. A coaching conversation could create the awareness for the leader that they were accepting assignments from their subordinates.

The manager feels the pressure to run the project, to perform the best, to control communications and innovations—and they end up unable to grow and focus on their own strengths. They're too busy doing everyone else's job. They *have* to, in this kind of company. Of course, they feel stuck. They're not growing, they can't add new talent, there are no openings for new opportunities or creativity. Their job might not be as much at risk as others' (although remember, no guarantees), but when anyone is let go, the manager takes over their workload. That's exhausting, and they have to dig their fingernails even further to control their team—which is, of course, a vicious cycle. There's a resignation at their level: "This is as good as it's going to get. This is what I have to do. This is the way it has to be..."

For ten years, I was an internal coach at a Fortune 10 company. I was the head of a community of practice numbering '450 internal coaches'. These people were not exclusively coaches, but it was a portion of their role; they used peer coaching or coached as a leader in their daily work. I was the only person who was exclusively a coach. I heard and saw a lot during my time there.

A coach plays a lot of different roles for different people. It's part confessional; I listened to the same stories again and again and again. It's also part-contributor: I helped develop business plans. People could think out loud with me, bounce ideas off me, confide in me when they had no one else to trust. The unique thing about a coaching relationship is that your coach doesn't have an agenda. If someone tells me, "I want to quit my job," I don't have to be invested. I can ask honest questions: "Tell me about that. Why would you quit your job? What's going on there?"

In 2015, I left that company to become an external coach. Now, I'm not tied to one company; I work with a lot of different people in different industries, especially the leaders. Executives often feel there's no one they can trust, which is where I come in. They can't share their ideas with their superiors because they're worried about that relationship. They can't share their ideas with their subordinates because they're trying to put on a good face. Not to mention, they don't know how the individuals will use the information either against each other or against them. A coach relationship is entirely confidential; my job is to partner with you. Coach Carl Dierschow shared that when he works with leaders, he helps them understand the benefits of opening up to employees and even in personal relationships, such as family—"because usually, other aspects of preserving the relationship take over the ability to be open and vulnerable. People resonate with that a lot."

> **TIME**
>
> According to the research done by the Human Capital Institute (HCI) and the International Coach Federation (ICF), the number-one deterrent to implementing a coaching culture is a lack of time. This perception of a lack of time seems to also apply to the individual manager or leader providing coaching. However, consistent feedback from my clients who are leaders, and other coaches who are training leaders in coaching skills, has shown that although coaching may take more upfront time than the 'tell, sell, yell' technique so many drivers prefer, the total time invested is much smaller in the long run.
>
> Michael Nunemaker, a leadership development program manager and coach in a US government organization, shares this anecdote: One of their frontline managers, Ed, had an employee who would routinely, seeking validation on a technical issue, take up 3 hours a week of this manager's time. But once the leader was trained in coaching skills, he learned how to create a true dialogue, and this time paradigm completely changed. Instead of 3 hours a week, he was still visiting regularly—but for 10 minutes, not three hours. Michael refers to this leader as his poster child, due to his enthusiasm and evangelism of coaching skills for leaders.

Most businesses, as you might have guessed, do not utilize this kind of coaching. Most companies do not build a coaching culture. The manager decides what needs to be done and how; the manager is compelled to provide far more oversight and control over the employee's process, output, and even how it is portrayed. The employees are intimidated and constantly afraid of punishment. There's no room for experimentation or failure. There isn't, in the end, a lot of room for creativity and innovation in that kind of environment.

On the other hand, in a coaching culture, a lot of that can happen in the conversation. You go through the questioning, the design, the outcome, the whole process, with a deeper level of tolerance. It's safe to fail. In the organizations without that coaching culture, it's definitely not safe to fail. It's reason for a pink slip.

Managers feel so much pressure to be right, to look right, that it becomes either faster or cheaper to just tell people how to do something. They can't risk taking the time to investigate or explore. Think of a time you've had an idea, and you try to train someone else to implement it. It's often easier just to say, "Forget it—I'll do it myself!"

The manager doesn't have time for a coaching culture because he's doing everybody else's job for them. And no one is happy about it. In Michael Bungay Stanier's book, *The Coaching Habit*, he offers that you can coach using 7 great questions in under 10 minutes!

CURIOSITY & CULTURE

Curiosity is a big word in coaching. When a leader, a manager, a company, becomes curious, they're willing to explore alternatives, and they're willing to learn through failure. People are more ready to be honest. Employees and managers alike learn to be curious and not judgmental about one another's opinions. They learn how to build each other up and create a better product. Retention improves significantly because they are not just focused on meeting a bottom line; the process of reaching goals is more comfortable, enjoyable, and conducive to creativity. Culture and their product turns around.

"Culture," in a company, is made up of the norms of behavior for any given organization. A Coaching Culture can have effects on every area, but it's important to remember you can have lots of subcultures based on geography or department or field. One of my clients once had an entire team of engineers in India helping on a huge project; oversight was coming from the United States, and there were some important cultural differences. They would have checkpoint meetings to ask for updates, and the group in India would assure them everything was on time. Culturally, in India, it's more important to be polite and agreeable than it is to be accurate. So even though the timeline was never going to happen, and they knew that way ahead of time, they never admitted it. They felt like it would be disrespectful to the leaders; whereas, culturally, here in the US, accuracy is important. That's an extreme example, but I think that each company has their own internal culture activities of what they do and how they behave based on that.

"So how can we address these differences? Judith E. Glaser's 'double-click' for meaning and understanding could be a tool used to uncover this cultural difference or applying the ICF core competencies, such as building trust, and co-creating the goals and deadlines as a project team. If team members and leaders are in a state of trust, more questions can be asked—that we don't know the answers to—which prompts more creative thinking. Again, this may raise the question of 'how much time will this take?' To avoid missed deadlines, and late customer deliverables, the time and relationship must be built upfront.

One of the exercises I do as a coach with teams is: "Visit Our Village" which comes from the wonderful resource, *Retreats That Work* by Liteman, Liteman, and

Campbell (see references worksheet). We pretend that we are anthropologists that have been dropped into the rainforests of Brazil, and have come upon on a new tribe that we've never discovered before. We ask them all kinds of questions of the organization: Who are the elders? What are the rites of passage? What do we go to war for? It's amazing to hear the answers that these people provide. I debrief with the leaders, and they're always shocked. They don't understand. "What do you mean that it's not safe? What do you mean that they won't support me?" They have no clue that this culture has developed beneath them. Culture can be explicit—published in company literature—or simply inherited based on how the leader operates, how coffee breaks go, how communications trickle down.

New leaders especially fall prey to this. They don't realize that they have a different management style than the last leader. They just assume that everyone will fall in line, even though the team has no idea what they're thinking. It's not unlike how we operate with romantic partners: we expect them to know what we're thinking, even if we never say it out loud.

> ### EXERCISE: CULTURAL VALUES
>
> When I do my coaching work with organizations outside of the U.S., I actually seek to embrace our differences, rather than homogenize them. I look to illustrate differences and within them find commonalities. The document I refer to again and again is "Values Americans Live by" by L. Robert Kohls who was the Executive Director of the Washington International Center in Washington, D.C. He wrote this document in April 1984, and yet it breathes true today. In this paper, he identifies unique American values, that could be mistaken for rudeness or aloofness by other countries that practice hospitality so well. By highlighting these, it allows others to identify their own values and how they are demonstrated. This rich discussion brings the group closer together and creates a vocabulary for collaboration.

ARE YOU READY TO CREATE A COACHING CULTURE?

So now, you've found this book. Maybe you're a new leader; maybe you're a manager who wants a change. You think this whole coaching culture might be the solution, and for a good reason. But I have to warn you: the number one principle here is the willingness to question your beliefs. If you've been walking around thinking it's faster and more effective to just tell people what to do, you'd better be ready to question that if you're going to keep reading. It comes down to embracing curiosity over judgment, which is traditionally the hardest leap for managers to make. It will be so tempting to keep telling your team, "This is how I did it. This is what worked for me, so go do it my way." That can even feel like coaching, but it's advising. Coaching is about asking questions without knowing the answer. Are you up for it?

Your whole life, you have been paid for the value you bring based on judgment. You went to school, you were trained in this, you know these things, and therefore you can decide what's best. That's how you've always done it. That's what you get paid for. But that's not coaching, and that won't create a coaching environment. Your whole life, you've been rewarded for judgment, and now I'm asking you to suspend judgment altogether. That, I promise you, will be difficult. Our brains are wired, are fighting, to be right. A lot of our ego and self-esteem has to do with being right. But do not confuse a *lack of knowing* with *being wrong*. It is not wrong to question with honest curiosity.

The average manager has about twelve employees. If you have to be right all of the time, all the answers you provide come from only one brain instead of twelve. You are cutting off a huge opportunity. If your team decides there's a better solution, you have to be willing to let them try it. You have to be willing to say "What if?" As Coach Ed Nottingham relates "The IQ of a group is always higher than that of an individual. Even an exceptional leader."

I've presented the data that shows that companies with a strong coaching culture outperform their peers financially and enjoy stronger employee engagement, higher retention, and higher productivity (see p. 4). I know that isn't enough for organizations to make the shift because the data still shows that the deterrents for implementing a coaching culture like a lack of time, an inability to measure ROI, and funding are still there. (HCI & ICF). So, continue with me, because in the next section of this book, I'll introduce the transformation of company culture that produces a higher retention and productivity rate. Not only that, but an engaged and excited workforce that is eager to produce new ideas, innovations, and creativity, a less overworked leadership team, with greater accountability and innovation from your subordinates.

If you're ready to question, to explore, to be curious, and take on the mantle of a 'culture change agent' so that you can build a coaching culture in your business, then you're ready to keep reading.

PART I: THE WHAT

CHAPTER 1:

WHAT IS COACHING

The International Coach Federation (ICF), the governing body for professional coaches, both accredits training programs and certifies individual coaches. They have created the body of knowledge that defines the Coaching Code of Ethics (after glossary) as well as the Coaching Core Competencies. (see break out on p. 27) The ICF standard definition of coaching is "partnering with clients in a thought-provoking and creative process that inspires them to maximize their personal and professional potential, which is particularly important in today's uncertain and complex environment. Coaches honor the client as the expert in his or her life and work and believe every client is creative, resourceful and whole. Standing on this foundation, the coach's responsibility is to:

- Discover, clarify, and align with what the client wants to achieve
- Encourage client self-discovery
- Elicit client-generated solutions and strategies
- Hold the client responsible and accountable

This process helps clients dramatically improve their outlook on work and life while enhancing their leadership skills and unlocking their potential."

I like to think of it as a co-created partnership where the coach and the client are working together to achieve the client's goals. They're equal partners, so there's no subordinate-superior relationship. The coach is an expert in the coaching conversation. The clients are the experts of themselves. The coach doesn't need to know anything about the client's subject field—their job is to ask questions to reveal the client's own wisdom.

PERFORMANCE MANAGEMENT VERSUS COACHING

If I am an equal as a coach, how can I be an effective leader? The coaching conversation is one that is appropriate for aspirational and open-ended thinking. The leader/manager conversations that involve a directive, usually referred to as performance management, are not coaching conversations. A leader can move back and forth between roles or simply incorporate the coaching skills within the conversation. The important piece is that when coaching, the coach does not have an agenda; in performance management, we do. We'll cover this in more detail in Chapter 10.

LEADER'S ROLE

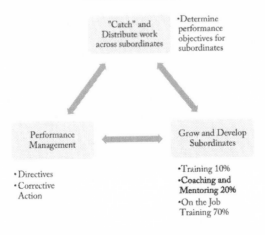

"Catch" and Distribute work across subordinates

•Determine performance objectives for subordinates

Performance Management

•Directives
•Corrective Action

Grow and Develop Subordinates

•Training 10%
•Coaching and Mentoring 20%
•On the Job Training 70%

Benefits to this process include greater ownership of the solution. Often when we get advice from other people, if we don't like it we don't explain why. We don't work through it; we just don't do it. The advisors have no ownership of it; they might not even be aware. If, on the other hand, we come up with our own idea, we're usually more excited about it and more prone to move forward. The coach's role is to ask those pointed questions, the questions that inspire the client's own genius. Then it's their idea, and they're passionate about it. At that point, the coach's role becomes one part cheerleader and one part accountability partner. We check in: If you said you were going to do this and you haven't yet, what's going on?

Sometimes, we get into unpacking elements of fear. That's when we have to uncover those hesitancies, those insecurities; we break it down into baby steps so the client can feel more comfortable. Sometimes they just need a pep talk!

Whatever the focus, the two most important aspects of having a coach are:

> A.) The coach doesn't have an agenda. They're there to serve the client.
>
> B.) They're not held back by the *limiting beliefs* that the client has.

WHAT ARE LIMITING BELIEFS?

A limiting belief is a limitation we impose on ourselves. It's not necessarily something logical in terms of an obvious obstacle; it's a belief that, whether subconscious or not, we treat as fact and limit ourselves accordingly. An example is the belief that 'women can't be doctors.'

There was a time period when, if you were a woman, you could not become a doctor. You had to be a nurse. This rule was in place because enough people believed it to be literally true; that women physically, mentally, or emotionally could not operate as a doctor of medicine. Now, even though the rule has changed and there are countless examples of female doctors who are quite successful and skilled, there are still people walking around with that belief in their head. The rule changed; the belief is somewhat stickier.

It's not logical whatsoever. In fact, a limiting belief rarely is. Often people don't even realize that they're allowing these beliefs to control them—the job of the coach is to uncover that. We create the awareness necessary for that person to say, "I'm holding myself back because I don't think it's possible for me to do this."

THE COACHING CONVERSATION

All trained and ICF certified coaches follow the ICF's Eleven Core Competencies. These are set out in the agreement with the client about what you're going to work on, not only for the entire engagement of your time together but also for each session.

First of all, for each session, the client always decides on the agenda. It's never the coach's job to decide precisely what you're going to talk about, but it is our responsibility to make sure there's focus for the session.

THE CORE COMPETENCIES

The Core Competencies are grouped into four clusters according to those that fit together logically based on common ways of looking at the competencies in each group. The groupings and individual competencies are not weighted—they do not represent any kind of priority in that they are all core or critical for any competent coach to demonstrate.

A. Setting the Foundation

  1. Meeting Ethical Guidelines and Professional Standards

  2. Establishing the Coaching Agreement

B. Co-creating the Relationship

  3. Establishing Trust and Intimacy with the Client

  4. Coaching Presence

C. Communicating Effectively

  5. Active Listening

  6. Powerful Questioning

  7. Direct Communication

D. Facilitating Learning and Results

  8. Creating Awareness

  9. Designing Actions

  10. Planning and Goal Setting

  11. Managing Progress and Accountability

Another part of the coach's role is to build trust and intimacy. I know 'intimacy' sounds like a funny word for a professional relationship, but it just means that your rapport is strong enough for the client to feel confident while discussing delicate situations or issues of confidence. Once they've established that trust and rapport, the coach's job is to ask those powerful questions. The most powerful questions are the ones that you don't have an answer for: they are open-ended and forward-thinking.

It's very rare that a coach will ask a question about the past because we can't do anything about the past. When the coach makes observations or notices a pattern, their job is to make that observation unattached. We ask the client if that's accurate, or if it's just the coach's view—which ties into the role of Powerful Communication. Then, the coach summarizes or paraphrases what's been happening in an empowering way to the client. That's when the coach observes, "You've worked hard, and you deserve this," or something similar, to build up the client in that way.

The next part of the conversation is what we call Strategy and Designing Actions. Together, we examine all of the opportunities to solve the issue at hand for the client. What are all the avenues possible? What would each course of action look like? What might get in the way? Once they've determined a course of action, then we implement accountability. When are you going to finish that? A coach's job is to push them just like a sports coach might push them—we get them to run another lap. The athlete might believe they can't run any further, but the coach knows they have it in them. If the client says, "I'll call three people before we meet next," the coach might respond with a challenge: "What would it take for you to call those three people today—or three people *every* day?"

RUNNING THAT ADDITIONAL LAP

When a client achieves more than they believed they could, it unleashes the potential and possibilities the client has. It elevates their conceptions of what is possible. Both Sir John Whitmore, author of the classic, *Coaching for Performance* and 'The Coaching Conundrum 2016' report by Blessingwhite revealed this phenomenon in their respective researches.

During the following session, the coach will follow up with that homework. How did those calls go? Do we want to change anything about your tactics? Do you want to expand? Do you want to discontinue this strategy? The goal is to help them analyze it before a new agenda is reestablished.

COACHING THE WHOLE PERSON

Although my experience has been mostly career and corporate coaching, the reality is, it's all coaching. I've even done some relationship coaching because our agenda is always whatever is most important for the client at that moment. If their love life is a huge distraction for them, and they can't focus on their projects at work, that's usually the best use of time: to resolve that relational issue. A lot of people seem to think that there are no emotions in business coaching, but that couldn't be further than the truth. I've seen it all. Sure, often it's entirely focused on business goals, but if you're coaching the whole person, you're coaching the whole person. No one is a business-only automaton.

When my team and I enter a workplace to start a coaching program, the superiors will often make some suggestions. They have a reason they're bringing us in, and they want their employees to work on that. It might come from the client's manager, or it might be tied to a workplace assessment. We always present these topics to the client, the actual employee we're working with, and let them know the opportunities those imply. But it's their individual decision whether to address those suggestions. Sometimes they don't agree with the assessment results; sometimes they don't agree with their boss. I do always try and remind the client that it's in their best interest to please their leader—their boss, after all, determines their pay. If the leader thinks they need to work on executive communication, I do think they should make some effort there. But if they make the decision that they want to work with me on something else, that's fine—they set the agenda. If the sponsor asks me how it's going, I can only respond, "We're meeting. You'll have to talk to Joe about how the sessions are going." I can't reveal any content.

Confidentiality is one of those Core Competencies. Coaches never reveal what you discuss in your session. If I'm aware of what the manager wants the employee to work on, I can remind them of that. I can be present when the client updates their manager, but I will never provide a progress report to a manager that includes topics or details, only that we are meeting—and I encourage them to speak to their employee to learn more.

THE COACHING AGREEMENT

A coaching agreement functions similar to a contract—explaining the obligations and expectations of each party. I encourage companies to include their 'standards of business conduct' as an exception to the client's privacy. If an employee is engaging in unethical practices that violate the company's policies, it's important that the client knows the coach is not obligated to stay silent and will report them. I prefer to include it in my work with companies, and when I review the agreement with the employee, I explicitly, *but in a light-hearted way*, inform them that if they are embezzling money from the company, do not tell me, as I will report them.

COACHING, CONSULTING, COUNSELING, OR MENTORING?

There are three helping professions that are often confused with coaching in some capacity. *Consulting* is different from coaching in that the consultant is a subject-matter expert and they provide advice on that subject. You may also hire a consultant for that expertise to conduct some work on your behalf. A *counselor* is an expert in their trade, and they too may give advice, addressing something that is not going well, often rooted in the past. A *mentor* also gives advice as a subject-matter expert (at least with more knowledge than their mentee or protégé) and establishes a more personal relationship that has to do with the whole person and their style; often, a mentor will pick one or two protégés to shape and form.

Coaching is distinct from these in one very powerful way: all coaching agreements assume that the client is creative, resourceful and whole. We're not trying to fix something that's broken, (although we may work to manage weaknesses) and we have an orientation towards the future. A lot of managers, when trying to hire coaches for their employees, overlook this. If someone's not performing well, the management team wants to assign a coach basically as a last-chance-fix before they're fired. That's not always coaching; that's a manager's job. We call that corrective action, or performance management, and most coaches try to steer far clear of it. But if the management team has a sincere desire to see this person improve, some coaches will consider working with that client.

I had a client who was a female director. She was suffering from confidence issues and was surrounded by male peers. They were very confident, very assertive, and they assumed authority where she was seeking permission. They assigned me to 'fix her' because it was causing her a lot of emotional distress. She had an enormously high stress level just planning out how she was going to interact with her peers, rather than naturally being herself and being the genius that she was.

They had some strong ideas about how she needed to behave, but these ideas didn't come naturally to her. I agreed to take her on as long as they didn't use this to specifically tell her how to do her job, as long as it was about improving her confidence, and operating without this emotional distress—*that* was what we would consider a success. They agreed, and sure enough, she was able to turn it around. She thought she had to be as they were, but she didn't realize that her strength was in her uniqueness. Somehow, she had labeled her unique self as being wrong, when in actuality, the only place she was erring was in trying to be like them.

Ironically, she was much more capable than her male peers because she had a great deal of emotional intelligence—and frankly, they didn't.

WHEN THE COACH REFERS TO ANOTHER PROFESSIONAL

If a topic in a coaching conversation reveals that the client needs specific expertise, for example 'how to do something' the coach can make the observation that they are not a subject-matter expert (SME), and perhaps the client would benefit from seeking help from an SME. If the client agrees, the coaching conversation may shift to selecting an SME to work with. The same process may hold true if the client is seeking relationship help; the coach is not a therapist or marriage counselor—the coaching conversation may shift to the criteria for choosing a therapist to work with. The Code of Ethics for Coaches is very clear: they only practice coaching within the engagement if that is what is stated in the agreement, even if they are qualified to practice other helping professions such as counseling. A separate agreement must be created for non-coaching work.

KNOW WHAT YOU'RE LOOKING FOR

It's essential to know the difference between these four fields—consulting, mentoring, counseling, and coaching—because otherwise, you may not get what you need. A lot of 'coaches' out there just dole out advice, even though they're not consultants. If you want to hire a coach, make sure that's what you need—then make sure that's what you get.

	Mentoring	Consulting	Therapy/Counseling
Shares with Coaching	• Works towards the goals of the client, protégé, or mentee	• Works to complete a set upon goal or goals identified by the client • May uncover new goals previously unrealized	• Works to reach the client's goals • Uncovers limiting beliefs • Creates awareness • Unique qualifications and certifications for the profession
Differs from Coaching	• Mentor is a Subject Matter Expert (SME) • Provides advice • May have an their own agenda or goal	• Mentor is a Subject Matter Expert (SME) • Provides advice • May have an their own agenda or goal • May have their own proprietary system of doing things	• May be working to 'fix' a problem rooted in the past • May provide advice

When I work with my clients, one of the things we do is build their virtual Board of Directors. Every executive director or CEO has a board of directors that is filled with people they trust, who are experts in their field. There's a finance expert, a legal expert and so on. When coaching on an individual level, we line up the functions of your life—parenting, business, etc. Then we make a list of the people in your life that can give you advice on these subjects. This clarifies my role—I *won't* be giving advice. I'm going to be helping *you* decide what actions to take, and some of those actions might mean going to an expert.

COACHING FOR PERFORMANCE

Often, it seems like managers reserve coaching for the lower-performing staff. Remember, though, coaching is not about fixing someone—that's performance management. Coaching should be treated as a privilege; it should be reserved as a reward for your highest-performing employees. Top-performers too often are just rewarded with more work—why not reward them with coaching, instead?

Sometimes, though, those top performers are the ones perpetuating this idea. They have the perspective that they're too busy for coaching. They don't realize how powerful that coaching relationship can be in terms of choosing what to work on, and how to work on it. The coaching relationship is unique, compared to anything else you have in your life because the coach is unattached to an agenda; their purpose is to partner with you to achieve your goals. If I came home one day and told my husband, "I don't want to go to work anymore," probably the first thing he'd say is, "I don't think so" The coach would simply say, "Where is this coming from? Tell me more." Most people in your life have an agenda, they're invested in your choices—your boss, your spouse, your friends. That's not necessarily a bad thing; they're just too defensive of their position to explore it without a bias.

While coaches have many jobs, one of the most important is to help others achieve their goals. And, at times, unleashing that potential and ideas that will help them be happier and more successful. This is one reason why a manager cannot coach their own employees; the manager has an agenda. Of course, they could use coaching skills while they're working, and that has a lot of value, but it's not a coaching relationship. If the employee says, "I'm not going to work on this other project because it doesn't have funding; I'm just going to focus on these other two," the manager might be thinking to themselves, "You still have to do it because I'm still accountable for it!" As a coach, they wouldn't say that. They'd say, "Tell me more about the strategy. What do you think it will do for you?"

DIFFERENT KINDS OF COACHING

We've talked a lot in this chapter about individual coaching, one-on-one, but that's only one way.

Other types of coaching:

- Peer coaching
- Team coaching
- Group coaching
  - Masterminding
  - Large Audience/Webinar with a Coach Approach

Let's explain each briefly before expanding:

Peer Coaching is a type of *one-on-one coaching*, where the coaches are coaching one another typically for the purposes of coaching skills development, but it can be used for personal or professional coaching as well.

Other types of coaching:

Team coaching is where all participants report to the same manager and one coach coaches that whole team.

Group coaching is similar in that it's one coach over multiple people, but they're not on the same team. Groups are organized by affinity or affiliates—they have a common goal, such as work-life balance, or a common background such as female engineers.

Masterminding is another form of group coaching that employs a group dynamic where everyone plays a coach in that they are mutually committed to one another's success. These groups typically are 6-8 people in size but may have more depending on the format used.

Large Audiences & Webinars uses a coaching conversation flow, where you can pose the questions that create awareness and design actions, while the participants think through the answers on their own.

HOW TO THINK THROUGH THE COST OF COACHING

In evaluating the expenses of coaching, we must always consider the benefits. The benefits to the individual, the impact on their work, and the impact to the business's bottom line. In the HOW section of this book, we talk about measuring the results of coaching, but in the meantime, consider the benefits of one-on-one attention compared to being one of many. In your own experiences working one on one with a mentor or coach, how did you benefit? What about a classroom? And when does the classroom size begin to affect your personal results? It may be topic-driven. My experience has been that awareness of our own true intrinsic motivations and concerns are not revealed in the large format environment. What is that insight worth?

TEAM COACHING

In team coaching, traditionally the whole group works for the same manager. That's what defines the team, but it might also be a project team that comes from multiple organizations. They're getting coached together.

I would sit down with the team and say "We're going to build this (product). Let's talk about what that will look like." Part of our job is to understand their desired result and then discuss it, to make sure that we're incorporating everybody's opinions as appropriate. Then we'll talk about the values that they want to use to get there. What are the team roles? How will we keep the team motivated? Sometimes there's a conflict that needs to be negotiated; without a coach or a facilitator there, the loudest person wins.

An aspirational approach can be far more powerful than a problem-solving approach, as this taps into the more creative sides of our brains and also creates a more we-centric mindset with the team, as opposed to an attachment to one's personal ideas. Judith E. Glaser reveals more about this in her work *Conversational Intelligence*™.

Sometimes, team coaching is necessary when the leadership changes. There is a new manager, and the staff need help to work through that. We'll discuss the attributes of the previous leader, what we know about the new leader, and try to fill in the blanks in between. We'll work out how they want to interact with their new boss, i.e. Do you want to wait until you break a rule, or do you want to ask upfront?

MANAGEMENT OF CHANGE

Management of Change is a popular coaching topic in organizations due to the rate of change in many industries. William Bridges pioneered this work in his book *Transitions*. This work guides employees through anticipated cycles of change and gives them tools for coping and building resilience.

GROUP COACHING

A group coaching session has a similar setup as a team coaching session, but the members are associated by affinity or affiliation. Affinity means that they have a common goal; it's the topic of the session. It could be a work-life balance, office relationships, or something like that. Affiliation means the group has something in common. For example, it might be a group of women engineers. This doesn't mean that those women engineers won't work on a goal like work-life balance, it just means that the topic was not the strategy for forming the group.

A group session can be run a couple of different ways. The coach can set the agenda and advertise it accordingly: "Come to a coaching session about Productivity!" In those cases, I usually have a mini-lesson to open, on various productivity challenges, but then it's free discussion. That's more coaching-centered, but still with structure. You might also just let the group decide what they want to talk about. Everybody sets their agenda, and then you group similar ideas together. Maybe half the group wants to talk about time management, and another half wants to talk about negotiating salaries. I simply coach on each topic one at a time.

MASTERMINDING

A third group-coaching strategy, Masterminding, utilizes the coaching efforts of the *group*, not just the coach. In this case, the coach is the facilitator. We help structure how the rest of the team will work with each individual. One person at a time will choose a topic, then receive input from the entire group, not just the coach. They'll offer tools, advice, and encouragement until that individual's time is up, and then we move on to the next person.

LARGE AUDIENCES & WEBINARS

It is also possible to use a coach approach with a large audience. This operates mostly as a group coaching session, but the size of the audience means the coach has to make some adjustments. I've done group coaching with five hundred people at a time, and there's a lot of functional value there. Basically, I present the topic for the session, then I ask them the open-ended coaching questions you'd expect. "Where are you today with this topic? How are you interacting with it?" It's about helping them create awareness and then asking, "Where do you *want* to be with it?" I'm asking the coaching questions, but they're working through their answers to those questions on their own.

This strategy also works well with webinars; again, it's more outbound coaching rather than interactive. However, I have found that in these webinars, the chat function is popular and effective. Participants can ask direct questions in the chat box or questions tab, and the coach responds as appropriate. Other participants offer their tools and resources as well in the chat function, which builds a nice community—if they are regularly offered.

DETERMINING WHICH GROUP COACHING MODEL TO USE

All of the variations of the group model are effective, but some build greater rapport amongst members than others do. Is this a goal of your group coaching? What is the length of the group engagement? Will the topic continue throughout the series? Will there be peer learning opportunities outside the group sessions? Do the members share a goal? Are they prepared to help one another reach those goals? When I consult with organizations that plan to use group coaching, we use a decision tree to determine the goals of the organization to form the right type of group coaching for them.

OPEN-ENDED QUESTIONS IN COACHING

In any coaching situation, it's important to be careful you know what you're getting into. The difference between the good coaching and the bad coaching is that the bad coaching has already predetermined an answer. All the questions being asked are driving to that answer. Do you know what you're supposed to be? Do you know what's expected? Do you know how this manager thinks of it? Do you know what their preferences are? You're going to do it their way? It's not exploratory or open-ended.

Often, the driver for these closed questions is an agenda. With some training and supervision, the leader or inexperienced coach can develop these questioning skills to be much more powerful. They can learn to suspend bias and grow curiosity.   Good coaching uses open-ended questions such as: "What do you want to talk about?" The client responds and instead of the coach diving straight in to "fix," the coach follows with, "Tell me about that." We don't say, "What are your challenges?" because that's a leading question. We just say, "Tell me about that." One of the big misconceptions in coaching is the idea that these open-ended questions take longer than just telling someone what to do, but in the end, that's never true. It's just more work upfront to help them get on a smoother path.

Coaches will help the client think through the topic, goals, and options. Then, when a course of action is determined, the client is far more likely to take complete ownership of the plan. In addition, if that course of action doesn't go as planned, the client can always come back and say, "I know we discussed this, and it seemed like it was going to go well, but this happened. Can we talk about what we should do now?" The client feels safe in this process because they were not told, "Go do this." When that directive goes poorly, the client doesn't want to ask for help—they just want to blame the manager who ordered them around!

This is a challenge everyone has to overcome when learning about coaching. The leader is driven to produce results which come from effective direction and answers to their subordinates' questions. Often, subordinates can be frustrated with open-ended questions when looking for answers. They often expect the manager to know or to tell. Your whole career, you might have been paid for having good judgment. You're the one who told people to go right rather than left, choose this rather than that, be more efficient—it's all about being right. That is not the coaching strategy; if it were, coaches would be very limited in the industries we could work in.

Unfortunately, suspending that need to be right is difficult. Just last month I was teaching a brand-new group of coaches coming out of law and finance. They kept asking, "We can't give advice?"

"Nope," I responded flatly.

"What if the client's doing it wrong?"

"Nope."

"But what if they're making a mistake?!"

"Nope."

"What if—"

The answer is always 'nope.' They were looking for ways around it, but that's not coaching. That's consulting, or maybe mentoring, but it isn't coaching.

THE COACH IS A PARTNER

I offer a solution to those frustrated by not offering advice. The coaching competencies refer to 'asking permission when coaching in new or sensitive areas' as a form of building trust and intimacy with the client. I believe asking permission to share information also builds trust and intimacy. "Would you like to hear about my experience regarding ..." can be powerful. Remember, the coach is a partner, and it is of no benefit for the coach to withhold knowledge or valuable information regarding the client's goals. By asking permission before volunteering the information, it allows the client to retain control of the conversational direction and whether they might be overly influenced by your opinion or experience regarding the topic. Some of my clients will say, 'yes, please' and some will say 'not just yet, let's finish this thread and come back to that.' Either way, I'm fine.

Now that you understand the fundamental basics of what coaching is and the many variations in which it can be applied, let's get into the *why* of whether you should consider this methodology to save your leaders' time and effort, improve your financial performance and increase your employee engagement by building a coaching culture.

PART II: THE WHY

CHAPTER 2:

WHAT CAN COACHING DO FOR YOU

"Culture eats strategy for breakfast"

Peter Drucker

After 23 years in corporate life, I have worked for as many leaders as the years I had in corporate. I was exposed to a wide range of leadership styles based on the values of the team, my leader's personal values, the crisis of the moment, the business priorities, the latest and greatest management /leadership book, and the political landscape. I can assert without reservation that leadership using a coach approach is the superior leadership style. A leader using coaching skills:

- Reduces manager and leader workload by eliminating the behavior of directing how the employee completes their objectives—or even worse—using a tell-sell-yell technique to compel employees to perform

- Facilitates employee ownership of their own personally conceived strategic actions and the manager's job is to hold them accountable
- Encourages employees to innovate and submit new and risk taking ideas instead of always using the leader's ideas
- Reduces disciplinary actions and performance management issues due to non-performance or behavioral problems, as the employee has personally identified actions and timelines for goals
- Creates a motivating and engaging environment as coaching allows true motivators of autonomy, mastery, and purpose

REDUCING LEADER AND MANAGER WORKLOADS

If a manager or leader has successfully completed their duties, they have received their objectives from above and distributed them across their workforce. All of these objectives are included in each employee's job description and work plan. As conditions change and new priorities arise, the leader must re-prioritize and communicate effectively with their team members. The most critical factors for the leader to perform to have an engaged workforce are:

- Setting Employee Expectations
- Equipping the employee to perform the work

EXPECTATION VS. AGREEMENT

Coach Steve Chandler has a wonderful resource—an audio discussing the differences of expectation vs. agreement. He summarizes thus: "Creating agreements works wonders. Up-vibe your personal and professional relationships by learning to create agreements instead of expecting others to do things (and then being disappointed when they don't)."

When a leader has properly set expectations, and set agreements with their employees, it reduces their burden of telling employees not only what to do, but how to do it. Their fear-based, controlling method comes from not trusting the employee to complete their assignments. If the leader has clearly outlined what is expected and equipped the employee with the tools and training to complete the tasks, their only job is to support and hold them accountable. The role can be made even easier by holding regularly-scheduled meetings that serve as progress reports, and a portion of the meetings' agenda should include what the employee may need from the manager such as approval, introductions, authorization, funding and so on. This shifts the relationship from command and control to collaboration and partnership. When adding the coaching skills to these conversations, the outcomes always include a segment of employee development.

FACILITATES EMPLOYEE OWNERSHIP

The coaching conversation using the GROW model includes key elements of goal, reality, options and way forward. By conducting employee conversations using a coach approach, the meeting is focused on their goals, and the employee is the center of the conversation. This approach emphasizes the leader's soft skills such as active listening and open-ended questioning that propel the employee towards their goals. The leader is partnering with them rather than telling or compelling the employee to do something their way. In this partnership, the leader is completely unattached to their contributions and allows the employee to determine the course of action to move forward and allows them to set their own timelines for completing the work. (Which should consider the organizational objectives and deadlines, 'the what to do' that the manager has distributed). When the employee has conceived the plan and set their own goals, the leader then supports and encourages their stated objective and the development that comes with this action. This autonomy creates a pride of ownership with the employee and removes the obligation of ownership from the leader. Their confidence is buoyed knowing their leader is behind them supporting their development and performance.

ENCOURAGES INNOVATION AND RISK TAKING

In the coaching conversation, the creation of options to meet the goal, allows the employee to explore all of the different approaches to reach the goal. It may explore previously attempted strategies or the leverage of past successes. It may even include wild and audacious theories not already proven. In this area of the coaching conversation, the employee is allowed to explore the possibilities and stretch themselves for growth. This process examines the strengths of the employee and not only what is possible but what would be fun and enjoyable as well as producing the most desired result. This allows the employee to examine that engaging idea "to do what they do best every day," (one of the Gallup Q12 questions). By examining the options available and the possible barriers, it allows the employee to assess and evaluate risks to accept the best path forward. This is done with the leader's partnership and support, making it less likely to fail, and if the attempt does fail, it is safe to fail. This environment facilitates the greatest innovation, and ensures not all of the innovation is coming from the leader.

REDUCES PERFORMANCE PROBLEMS

Dave Packard wisely said, "there are no poor performers, only actors miscast in their roles." This was fueled by the belief that every employee wants to do a good job. When the leader embraces the coaching belief that the employee is creative, resourceful and whole, they assume the best. They approach the employee with the intent of building rapport. When a leader builds rapport with the employee, they make agreements that when fulfilled, help develop trust. The skills of active listening, and asking open-ended questions demonstrate that the leader trusts the employee to arrive at answers. When the employee feels trusted to arrive at their own answers, they build their confidence to come with their struggles and a request for help when needed.

The coaching conversation focuses on behavior and outcomes rather than being filled with the 'ask, then tell' logistics of progress reports. This allows room for the leader to focus on, and share what the employee is doing well. The leader has the opportunity endorse their strengths and values as they contribute to the employee's work product. This amplifies the employee's use of those strengths and manages their weaknesses.

This eliminates problems before they can emerge, and reduces the avoidance of difficult conversations that so many leaders are prone to. In the event of emerging issues, such as tardiness, ambiguous ethics, or colleague tensions, they can be addressed immediately—when the observation is first noticed rather than waiting for a pronounced pattern to emerge. Should behaviors need to be corrected, the manager can 'slip on their performance management hat' and set the expectation for proper behavior as a directive, but can immediately return to the coaching conversation in covering options for how to correct this, driven by the employee.

This conversation focused on the employee's solutions, demonstrates care for the person as well the work. In the coaching conversation, the employee's opinion always counts as that is what fuels the way forward. These coaching behaviors address Gallup's Q12 Engagement areas of receiving recognition, doing good work on a regular basis, being cared for as a person, someone at work encouraging development, and opinions counting—all addressed by shifting from a command control approach to the coaching conversation.

CREATES A MOTIVATING ENVIRONMENT

Earlier we discussed Dan Pink's work in *DRIVE*. Employees are motivated by autonomy, mastery, and purpose. When the leader uses the coaching conversation, the employee not only determines their path forward to execute their goals but also stretches their development, mastering their methods and craft. If the leader has properly connected the company and department objectives to the employee's plans, it also provides purpose. By feeling a connection to purpose, the employee feels their objectives are important. It creates a sense of interdependence that suggests their peers and others are depending on them and a quality work product is necessary. When all employees are committed to this excellence, it is motivating and inspiring, creating a healthy peer pressure to perform. When we feel we are aligned, it creates trust and often friendship.

When we arrive at work each knowing our role is important, it contributes to a higher purpose. And when our colleagues are also committed, we are inspired. We are committed to our own colleagues' growth and development, and we share learning and best practices to make the entire team better. The coaching conversation naturally has a support function; it endorses the employee's strengths and abilities while asking them to do more. These qualities are the same qualities that drive engagement.

OUTPERFORMS PEERS FINANCIALLY with HIGHER EMPLOYEE ENGAGEMENT

As we covered in the introduction, when an entire team, department, organization, or company builds a strong coaching culture, they outperform their peers financially, (Gallup and the HCI & ICF research) and enjoy higher levels of employee engagement which drives:

- Productivity
- Profitability
- Retention

APPLICATIONS FOR COACHING

A strong coaching culture is correlated with higher employee engagement and stronger financial performance. Our data shows that there are opportunities to outperform your competition financially by building a strong coaching culture and higher employee engagement. Employees who have an open dialogue with their management feel more connected to the business and more tied to the company results. They feel more empowered. They take more ownership of the solutions that they've personally been involved in designing, and they learn more when things go wrong. When the management team is involved and supportive, it's safer to fail.

THE PRISM AWARD

In 2005, The International Coach Federation (ICF) Global adopted the Prism Award, a concept developed by ICF Toronto to recognize outstanding organizational coaching initiatives. Today, the International Prism Award honors businesses and organizations with coaching programs that fulfill rigorous professional standards, address key strategic goals, shape organizational culture, and yield discernible and measurable positive impacts.

REDUCING DISCIPLINARY PROBLEMS IN SCHOOLS

As a five-time International and Chapter Prism judge, I've had the privilege to review outstanding demonstrations of coaching culture. In 2013, the International Prism Award winning Isikkent Schools of Turkey applied a coaching culture "using 24 percent of the school's professional development budget for coach training for teachers." More than 40 teachers took on addition-al training to enroll in a coaching program to become coaches. Coaching was then offered to anyone in the school community who wanted it. 'Disciplinary problems in the middle and high schools declined sharply since the introduction of coaching.'

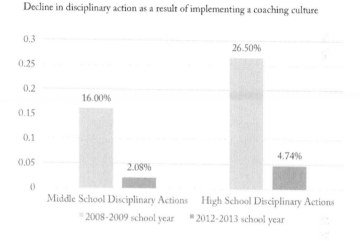

Decline in disciplinary action as a result of implementing a coaching culture

This is just one illustration of the many applications and business objectives that can be addressed with the building of a coaching culture. The Global and Local ICF Chapter Prism Award honorees include many small businesses and organizations like Isikkent Schools. The return on investment (ROI) and return on expectation (ROE) can be realized even more quickly with smaller populations and organizations. When effectively coach-ing a leader, who then brings new ideas and leadership styles to an organization, the application is felt by every-one downstream.

The coach approach embraces curiosity, strategy,

design, ownership, and accountability—with all organizations recognizing the impact. When this culture is embraced, it becomes part of the identity of the organization. As Peter Drucker said, "Culture eats strategy for breakfast."

TAKING MORE OWNERSHIP

Some unique applications that work well for the smaller business include: coaching employees to take more ownership outside the boundaries of their own role. Smaller organizations are more likely to have more white space between positions that need ownership for the company to produce its desired result. The employee then looks to the manager for guidance on taking the initiative rather than waiting for concrete direction. The more the manager can rely on individuals to show initiative and take ownership, the more free time the manager will have for themselves to work projects, as a smaller company is less likely to have leaders exclusively dedicated to management.

ONBOARDING NEW EMPLOYEES

Other applications include onboarding new employees. Coach Matt Becker of CareSource, a nonprofit managed care organization and a 2014 International Prism Award honorable mention, implemented coaching to onboard new leaders at his organization which has grown from 350 employees to over 3,100.

Inspired by *The First 90 Days* by Michael D. Watkins, Becker expanded coaching to include a one-day coaching skills course for the leadership team, who then became advocates to develop coaching to the front-line level of the organization; including it as one full day of their one week of training. The organization was satisfied with using return on expectation (ROE) to begin with and then later formalized measurements to include return on investment (ROI) at the request of the CEO, to correlate with their impact surveys. Becker states that coaching is 'critical to sustaining and spreading the culture of the organization.' Becker indicates that individuals who had received coaching demonstrated higher employee engagement in 14 of 15 key drivers.

EMPLOYEE RETENTION

The greatest return on investment for a large company is their intellectual capital: their people and their talents. The more that they can retain those top-performers, the better.

In speaking with Organizational Coach and Psychologist Doug Flor, he describes it this way: There are two types of top performers. First, there's what we call the breakthrough innovative entrepreneur-types. They get things done, and that's why they're valuable to the company. Secondly, there's the less ambitious type. These employees are more careful and considerate, but they're also deeply invested in their relationship to the company; they value the experience of being an employee rather than the ambition itself. Those are the people who often make the best managers. They're the ones who can nurture the talents of the first group, who can sandpaper off all the rough edges of those "barn-burners" (as we call them) and make sure that they get assigned to the ambitious projects that will keep them satisfied—but will also meet the company needs.

Coaching can work for both of these segments. It can work for the barn-burner type who may need to learn diplomacy; it can also work for the careful, considerate manager who might need to take more risks. Both of these employees are top-performers, but what drives the coaching will be different. With the barn-burner client, we'll be asking more about considering their blind spots. The coach will try and see if they have a balanced approach or not. This isn't to slow them down, but to help them see who they might have overlooked in their earnest desire to get things finished. Usually, they're moving so fast to achieve their goal that they don't notice who they've overlooked. They're the bull in the china shop. Every manager probably wants one of these, but they can offend people, which makes those same people less interested in working with them on future programs. So, the coaching goal is to help them see the value in "winning friends and influencing people," Dale Carnegie style, rather than driving over them to reach their goal.

The more careful or considerate manager, on the other hand, will more likely talk about risks in their coaching time. We'll explore their confidence, and why they might be leaning too heavily on one area to make decisions. The coaching strategies may be to help them do more things outside their comfort zone each day, to try new things, maybe even to think less and act more.

With both types of performers, by harnessing and utilizing their talents appropriately, they are more likely to feel valued, to contribute at a higher level, and to stay with a company due to their high level of engagement.

PERSONAL PRODUCTIVITY

For many, coaching is an opportunity to think out loud. Everyone's so scheduled; they're in back-to-back meetings all day long. They never sit back and reflect on why they're doing all of this in the first place. Sometimes, coaching is about maximizing productivity or acclimating to a new position. Frequently, when people move from manager to director, that's the first time they have their own dedicated administrative assistant. We'll talk about how to best utilize that assistant, what kind of tasks they want to have them do, and how to keep on top of it. What's going to be their methodology? How long before they review the process and say, "I want to make these changes?"

INCREASING SALES

Often, organizations will invest in coaching for their salespeople, because top-line growth can be a struggle for companies that are overly focused on infrastructure. Salespeople are notorious for big ideas and big thinking, but they're frustrated when it comes to the details. They often have poor time-management and productivity skills. For them, coaching is about finding a happy medium where they're not too weighed down by a process, but they still have everything on paper.

HIGH POTENTIALS

In speaking with leaders, one of their strongest motivators to create an internal coaching program is to support an underserved population—that of the high-potential first-line manager or leader. High-potential and high-level leaders are served by the external coaching programs, but those programs often do not reach down to the first levels of the organization, and those populations are frequently those who supervise or lead the highest number of employees. These tend to be younger and newer managers who may need more support that those who are more seasoned. They also tend to be a population that the company intends to grow and promote to higher levels as they mature in the company and their careers—why not provide them with coaching to build a strong leadership foundation?

CAREER MILESTONES

Ernst & Young (EY) began their amazing coaching program in 2010 under the leadership of Jackie Bayer. Eight practicing coaches from different parts of the company were brought together to form an in-house executive coaching team focused on coaching newly promoted partners. "Achieving promotion to partner is an amazing milestone, and cause for celebration as it's something these professionals have been working towards for years. Yet, it's also one of the most challenging transitions of their career with the significant increase in authority, ownership and visibility. Dawn Pons, Americas Director of Executive Coaching and Career Transitions, relates, "senior partners remember facing this challenge," and were supportive of the program.

The intention of the program was to help new partners get their footing faster, and accelerate their success. Dawn attributes much of their success to specialized in 'transition' coaching for the first several years. The experience gained in coaching over 3000 executives in transition led the team to develop intellectual property on what successful leaders focus on to thrive during transitions. This methodology has enhanced the coaching engagements within EY as well as gained external recognition. EY now has 23 full-time executive coaches based in the Americas supporting leaders during defining moments:

when they are in transition, leading a team and exploring their career future.

FOR THE CLIENT

Engaging in coaching does not necessarily mean you'll be promoted this week. It's important to remember that. That being said, the benefits for you as an employee are plentiful. Coaching provides clarity of thinking, a partner to bounce ideas off of, a revelation of blind spots. You'll leave with a greater understanding of your work within the context of that company. You'll build your own awareness of behaviors that support or detract from your performance. You'll be able to look at your strengths and your reputation to intentionally hone how you're known in the company.

It's easy to take the path of least resistance and forget about these kinds of opportunities, especially if you're overworked. If my client has to go to a week-long meeting and I ask about their goals, they might respond, "I'm just going to the meeting." They have to go, and they're not interested in getting anything extra out of it. But after some questioning, we find they are hoping to get to know the other department heads at this meeting. They have some interest in working in that department. So, why not have lunch with some of the folks at the meeting?

Coaching is about presenting those opportunities.

CHAPTER 3:

AN INTRO TO THE THREE MODALITIES OF COACHING

No two companies need coaching in the same way. Each company culture has its own history, its own issues, and its own performance to gauge and work through. Some of your needs may be dictated by the market, and some may be dictated by your competition. Just like in any business planning process, when you're planning for coaching, you'll go through your vision, mission, market, finances—everything. The coaching program will then be tailored to fit those unique needs.

There are three basic modalities when it comes to coaching. The first involves the external coaches coming into work with a company. These are trained, certified coaches completely independent of the company; they're contractors, not employees. These coaches tend to be more expensive, but they can also broaden the company's perspective and bring a more experienced skillset.

The second modality is training current managers to develop their coaching skills. This means they do other work for the company but can utilize their coaching skills as well. The benefit here is that this program is quite easy to implement and has the least amount of investment.

You do have to make sure there's follow-up training as well as some supervision, to ensure that the coaching skills are being implemented correctly, but once the system is established, it's extremely low-cost.

The third modality is hiring internal coaches. These coaches are directly employed by the company exclusively for coaching. They're part of the team, but they don't have other work responsibilities. This can be a very inexpensive solution compared to external coaches; however, these coaches can occasionally face potential conflicts of interest in confidentiality. I've been in situations where I'm coaching both the manager and the employee, but they don't know it. The employee might be stressed about a project that I know is already canceled, but I can't say anything. Those situations can be sticky, but there's still a lot of value with an internal coach who is already familiar with the company culture.

CHOOSING YOUR MODALITY

We don't know what we don't know. Understanding the coaching program that will work best for you is a process of discovery, of interviews, and of careful observation. The benefit of an outside coach is, of course, the outside eye. We've been in a lot of companies, we've seen how a lot of people work, and we can observe things that are unique to your business. Those might be assets that you want to extrapolate further, or they might be liabilities that you need to fix. Either way, when you're so internally focused, you can't necessarily see these things yourself. Collectively, the coach and the leadership can decide together how to focus the coaching engagement.

When the company leaders start with one-on-one

coaching, it will help them identify how they'll personally benefit from the program; with that understanding, they can be much better advocates for the coaching movement throughout the company. People can perceive coaching as corrective action rather than a privilege, but if they see that the leaders are involved, they're less likely to think of it negatively.

The next step is usually a one- or two-day workshop with all the leaders. There, you'll get an overview of coaching skills. It's a training workshop on the basics of healthy coaching, and how you can utilize it as leaders. Some companies have highly emotionally intelligent people who have assimilated this through years of experience, but in some places, this can bring about a real 'aha' moment. "I had no idea that I was intimidating!" or "I didn't realize I was cutting people off."

The biggest mistake that happens at this point is a lack of follow-up. After that workshop, it's essential to get some supervision by an experienced coach to confirm that they're performing these skills correctly. This can be a refresher training, an observation day, or a debriefing. I did a recording session once where I listened to a recording of the client and worked through it with him, using coaching questions. "You ask this question here. As the recipient of that question, where do you think their brain went?" "What other questions could you have asked that would be more open-ended, have less of an agenda?" We encourage them to practice peer coaching and consistent feedback.

After this process, you'll be at a place where you can understand more fully where a coaching culture could fit in at your company. Then you can decide whether you want to have exclusively external coaches, whether you simply want to keep training your leaders and managers, or whether you want to make a long-term investment and hire some internal coaches.

HIRING INTERNAL COACHES

When it comes to internal coaching, there are two schools of thought: Hire from within, or hire from without. You can find someone who is already a coach and hire them full- or part-time at your company, or you can promote from within and send an employee who has potential to be certified as a coach.

If you choose the latter option, you'll also have to decide whether they're going to coach full-time or split their current duties with their coaching duties. The challenge there, of course, is you never want to coach anyone in your own department. They might be too close to it, they'll have their own agenda and conflicts of interest, and there will be confidentiality issues.

There are mixed views when it comes to hiring someone from HR to become a coach. If an employee mentions in a coaching session that they don't like their manager, what happens the next time that HR person is present in a conversation *about* that manager? Can they remove themselves in that capacity and not speak up? It puts them in a difficult position, and the employees end up not trusting their coaches in the way they need to.

The kind of employee that's usually ripe to pursue coaching is someone who's always been interested in the people aspect of their job. They're the ones leading employee initiatives, volunteer days, or Bring-Your-Child-To-Work day. Sometimes they're the ones that lead the plans for employee surveys. They'll be highly interested in any sort of 'people' topic. If you look at the Myers-Briggs Personality Type, a lot of coaches are what they call the counselor—an INFJ. They love people, but they're introverted; they prefer that one-on-one or small group dynamic; they tend to be thoughtful listeners. Then again, it doesn't always have to be the person with the raw natural skillset. If someone already has a lot of respect from their peers and they're a leader, they might be effective coaches, too.

PART III: THE OPTIONS

CHAPTER 4:
EXTERNAL COACHING

"Does coaching work? Yes. Good coaches provide a truly important service. They tell you the truth when no one else will."

JACK WELCH, FORMER CEO OF GENERAL ELECTRIC

In this chapter, we'll cover the details, benefits, and drawbacks of working with external coaches

An external coach, as we touched on before, is brought on from outside the company. They're not employees; they're independent contractors. External coaches can come in at any level of the organization. They may be hired to provide workshops, one-on-one coaching, or coach training, but most commonly it's used for the C-suite. In a large corporation, the C-suite are the Vice-Presidents and above—the higher-ups. The benefit of external coaches here is they can introduce new ideas. Companies tend to focus inwardly, but with an external coach, they've got a fresh perspective. Many coaches are former execs themselves; there's even the opportunity for occasional mentoring if it's appropriate. It's important to distinguish that mentorship from coaching; coaching should never be about advice. If the client asks a question and the coach has the ability and resources to answer, from their own experience, they can open up about that, but they'll need to make the transition to mentor first. Coaches need the formality of their training to establish appropriate boundaries and observe the code of ethics. The Core Competencies apply to any level of coach. As a reminder, the core competencies are 11 key skills that a coach practices when working with clients including building trust and intimacy, designing actions, and managing progress and accountability.

The biggest disadvantage of external coaching is the expense. Coaching, depending on the region, can range from $400- $1000's an hour. When speaking to those hiring external providers, most mention an average of around $650 USD/hr. A lot of external coaches have a relatively high billable rate; I've seen it get up to $6,000 a day with top executives. *(This is about 6x the rate of an internal coach)* Then again, if the coach is bringing in a workshop, they're bringing in their experience as well as all of the research and preparation that went into the workshop. The external coach, to that end, can also be occasionally flexible on budget—you can 'order' as much or as little as you need. Maybe you only meet a couple of hours a month; maybe you work with one executive for a week. You can adjust to your budget.

The flexibility is also important for those in small or micro businesses. An internal coach is difficult to justify due to the small circle of people, but having an external coach on retainer can make good financial sense.

> "Even modest improvements can justify hiring a coach. An investment of $30,000 or so in an executive who has responsibility for tens of millions of dollars is a rounding error."
>
> —JEROME ABARBANEL,
> VP OF EXECUTIVE RESOURCES, CITIBANK

FACTORS TO CONSIDER IN HIRING THE EXTERNAL COACH

When Christine Barnes, Director, Organization Development at Oracle, was seeking to standardize their existing external coaching program in 2013, she was eager to address three main areas: controlling costs, ensuring professional standards and obtaining oversight of the performance of the program. These areas are important for all businesses seeking to begin an external coaching program and worthy of discussion here.

CONTROL COSTS

It is important that a budget is set for the external coaching, and the vendors the organization is working with can provide consistent delivery for a reasonable price. The easiest way to understand the market is to put out a request for proposal.

ENSURE PROFESSIONAL STANDARDS

All of the participating coaches should be accredited (i.e. ACC, PCC, or MCC with the ICF), have experience coaching in your type of business, practice the ICF code of ethics, and practice the ICF core competencies. The entire body of coaches providing coaching should use the same documentation (coaching agreements, reporting tools, etc.) These conditions can help ensure a standard level of quality in the coaching experience.

REPORTING: PERFORMANCE AND TRACKING

All coaches should be reporting sessions with their clients into a database. The dates and times are sufficient, naming the topic of discussion would violate the practice of confidentiality.

REASONS TO BRING IN EXTERNAL COACHES

"Business coaching is attracting America's top CEOs because, put simply, business coaching works. In fact, when asked for a conservative estimate of monetary payoff from the coaching they got... managers described an average return of more than $100,000, or about six times what the coaching had cost their companies."

– FORTUNE Magazine

KEEPING IT CONFIDENTIAL

Another reason C-suite execs tend to work with external coaches is the need for confidentiality. Now, it doesn't matter if you're an internal coach or an external coach, ethics always requires complete confidentiality in the coaching sessions. Sometimes, however, an executive might be debating a decision that could affect an internal coach. They won't be able to effectively coach; it will be almost impossible to remove themselves from their agenda of staying employed.

The topics executives want coaching on tend to be big-picture issues. They need a partner to guide them through problem-solving when it gets too complicated; sometimes, they need someone to help them develop their executive skills or presence. Either way, Executives want to know that the coach is more invested in *them* than in the company.

Coach Carl Dierschow explains confidentiality to his clients in this way "Everything is confidential until it comes to illegal, immoral, or in violation of company standards." He says clients can understand why each of these exists; it seems fair, and it's reasonable. It's consistent with ICF and legal requirements in the USA.

EMPLOYEE SURVEYS AND ASSESSMENTS

Often, when companies do an employee assessment, they'll bring in an external coach to help interpret the results or develop an action plan. The coach's job here is to make sure the subject of the survey understands the data, and what it means. They have to determine for themselves whether they agree with that and whether they want to do something about it.

Frequently, companies can be reticent when it comes to difficult conversations. They use the assessment as an excuse to shuffle their problems off onto a coach; they only do the assessment to have an excuse to tell a leader about their poor communication skills. Then, they hire the coach to do the telling—sometimes these people need to be hit with a figurative two-by-four because they just don't believe it. They think they're doing great! Then again, often the assessment will reveal a problem the company didn't even know they had; a coach can help with that, too.

USING ASSESSMENTS TO CREATE AWARENESS

When a leader truly understands and agrees with the feedback, changes can happen at a much deeper level and with greater speed. This acceptance of the feedback demonstrates presence and a sense of accountability with the leader to make lasting change. While external coaches may advocate for specific assessments, they are partial to, internal coaches share that their organizations tend to be agnostic when it comes to assessments, but members of their team may specialize and perform assessments for clients of other coaches to reduce costs in the company.

EXTERNAL PERSPECTIVE

As I mentioned before, a company can get so stuck in their own navel-gazing that they can't see the solution right in front of their face. They're staring inward; they're too close to the problem. An external coach is a perfect solution for that. Maybe an organization is focused on bringing a product to market, but they're not considering customer perspective; maybe they're so focused on the customer perspective, they're missing key cost issues. They keep running the numbers again and again to tell the story that they've already told themselves. A coach can break up that cycle.

IDENTIFYING THE TRUE PROBLEM

A coaching colleague of mine did some work with a regional corporation, which brought her team in to address what they thought was a pay-grade issue. The employees were not being respectful and were abusing the system. Examples of this disrespect and abuse included helping themselves to small-priced merchandise, and not tidying up after themselves in the employee restrooms. But, once the coaches got in there and did all the interviews with the employees, it turned out the problems had nothing to do with pay. It was actually about the employees' inability to see their own career path. Once the coaching team had helped this company identify career paths for all of the existing positions, the poor behavior corrected itself, because they felt valued and part of the larger team.

FRESH EYES

Sometimes, companies can also have a problem with 'case histories.' They have employees who've been there so long that they won't change their perceptions, despite the changing realities. They keep thinking of rules or cultures as the same old thing. A woman I worked with, for example, started as a secretary at a company. Over a period of twenty years, she worked her way up and up until she was a director. One day, I was having a conversation with a sales person. I referred to this woman, and he replied, "You mean the secretary?"

I was shocked. It had been twenty years! Perceptions can be slow to change.

If one person can do that, you can imagine how an entire company culture can become mired in doing it the way 'they've always done it.' They don't recognize that they need to make a shift; the external coach can help them see it.

KEY PLAYERS FOR EXTERNAL COACHES

HUMAN RESOURCES (HR)

Tasked with bringing innovations in human capital to the organization. When introducing coaching to their organization, they may be trying to solve a problem or keeping up with trends and case studies in the marketplace. They, more than most, understand the millennial generation's driver to develop via relationships. (I believe our traditional experiential learning pyramid of 70/20/10 mix of on-the-job training, relationships, and classroom training, will shift dramatically in the next ten years to a 40/40/20 mix due to the millennial influence.) HR often acts as the gatekeeper to the relationship with external coaches or talent management brokers of coaching.

EXECUTIVES

Always on the lookout for what is happening in the marketplace around them, peer conferences and network contacts share coaching as a must. Most executives are coached by external coaches for the benefits of mastery and experience of the external coach—many are former executives themselves—and for the extra layer of confidentiality that allows them to speak freely regarding business changes that may affect an internal coach. These executives are swift to see the benefit that coaching may bring to the organization particularly in the areas of retaining high-potential talent, retaining newly recruited employees, or helping those new to a level acclimate to the stepped-up challenges of the new role. Executives are the most likely to desire Key Performance Indicator (KPI) measures and Return on Investment (ROI) or Return on Expectation (ROE). *Some of the major accounting firms around the world use coaching—and ROE is good enough for them.*

INTERNAL COACHES

This may be a trained coach that is already an employee of the company who wants to share their skill set and value add with the organization, but at executive levels through external coaches. These coaches make proposals of internal pilots to grow the portion of their role that uses coaching and attempts to make this a formal part of the organization to solve business challenges.

The introduction of coaching by an executive or HR may be a bit smoother rather than trying to push for approvals at lower levels, but in any case, the project management must be strong. The expectations for the program must be well-defined, and key performance indicators (KPIs) baselines well-established. If you are trying to improve retention or sales performance, you must understand where you are today to realize if you have arrived at where you want to be.

The interesting challenge of these three perspectives in introducing coaching is that they often don't have a full understanding of one another's challenges and desires around coaching. The internal coach doesn't have a full understanding of the executive's numbers and headcount controls. The HR partner doesn't always understand that surrendering a resource to coach means there is one less project manager or engineer to execute on projects. To gain a full understanding, all the parties need to be involved in planning.

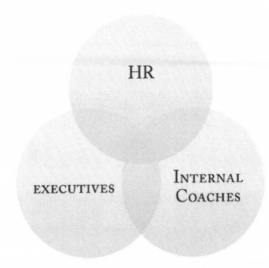

With external coaching, the key players involved are usually HR, and the executives themselves. They're the two most likely to get the process started. The executives might go to some kind of external training, networking, or industry event, where they hear about coaching. Maybe they run into a colleague who's been working with a coach, and who's had a great experience. Ironically, a lot of executives will brag about their coaches, because it's a perk that comes with their role; they know the value of it. Internal, lower-level folks, however, are sometimes embarrassed to receive the same perk, believing it is some variety of remedial help

When the executive hears the good review for coaching, they decide to try it and find a way to open the company's purse strings. They try it, they love it, and then they think everybody should have it.

The same sort of thing might happen with HR. They go to a conference and hear about the latest greatest thing, which for the last few years has been coaching. They bring it back and suggest it to their own team; they become the influencers.

The trick is, you have to experience it. You can talk about coaching until you're blue in the face and people just won't get it until they truly experience it.

WHO BENEFITS FROM EXTERNAL COACHING?

You've got to pick the modality of coaching that's best for you, and in my experience, external coaching works on both ends of the bell curve. For all the reasons I already stated, the bigger companies can benefit from coaching for their C-suite. But the benefits for smaller companies, who can't afford to hire a full-time internal coach, are great, too. For example, a coach that works with a local bank that has twelve employees; they can't afford to bring in an internal coach! That would be 1/13th of their payroll. But hiring a coach for a few hours a month? That makes sense. An additional reason to bring in an external coach for the small business: objective distance. With such a small population, it would be difficult for the internal coach to take on the mantle of 'external independence' in any given situation.

> "I never cease to be amazed at the power of the coaching process to draw out the skills or talent that was previously hidden within an individual, and which invariably finds a way to solve a problem previously thought unsolvable."
>
> JOHN RUSSELL, MANAGING DIRECTOR,
> HARLEY-DAVIDSON EUROPE LTD.

However you decide to bring in an external coach, finding a good fit is essential. A lot of talent brokers will have a pool of executive coaches with profiles for you to look through; you can also certainly meet or interview the coach before you hire them. If you don't connect with the coach you choose, the whole thing will be a waste of time.

According to Stephan Wiedner, COO of Noomii.com, a talent broker and referral service for coaches on the web, their goal is to match every coaching client, whether it be a C-Suite executive of a Fortune 500 company or a manager of 12-person bank, with their ideal coach. They recommend coaches based on the client's position, seniority, and stated goals. Although some coaches appear to have the perfect background and training for a given client, their personalities may not mesh. For that reason, it is critical that the client interview two or three coaches to determine the best fit.

Brian O. Underhill, Ph. D. Founder and CEO of CoachSource, an executive coaching partner, works with clients to ensure a fit for their scope of work and budget, experience and standards of their coaches and any reporting needs they may have.

FISH-TO-TABLE

As a panelist judge of the ICF Vancouver Prism Awards, we were presented with an application from a company that demonstrated large impact with few people. They were a small, grassroots business that wanted to connect small-scale fishing families and their sustainable catch to consumers; they wanted to take the farm-to-table idea and make it fish-to-table.

They started with only one coach, Brad Herbert (PCC) and one client: Sonia Strobel, Co-Founder & Managing Director of Skipper Otto's Community Supported Fishery.

The coaching partnership focused on leveraging a clear organizational mission, dedicated to social justice, to grow her business.

During this engagement, the client developed key skills instrumental to her success like vulnerability, asking for help, reflection, and gratitude. Although the client and her community were new to the business, they developed a conscious and collective leadership approach, which allowed them to partner with the local community in innovative ways and created a culture for their fish to table movement. The client then took on a leadership role for LocalCatch.org and their summit for North American Community Supported Fisheries (CSFs).

The transformation in the business has been outstanding: at the time of the application, the membership had grown in the CSF from 634 to 2,117 members. (233%). Employment grew from 3 to 12 persons, and participating fisherman grew from 10 to 30. The fishermen are paid, on average, 30% more than they can get anywhere else.

The client now earns 300% more than when coaching began. She has generated visibility through national press releases from tier-one media outlets to increase distributions to new channels, including a retail co-op partnership and Canada's first Restaurant Supported Fishery, championed by celebrity Chef Ned Bell.

Between one business owner and one coach, they created a partnership and a plan that affected the lives and the livelihoods of thousands. By setting the goals of the engagement such as clarifying personal and corporate values, and using company values to make long-term strategic decisions, they were able to achieve the client's goals of the company mission and dedication to social justice.

That's how external coaching can help smaller companies, just as much as the bigger fish out there (pun intended). If you write the contract within budget, you can work with what you can afford. There's no benefits or payroll to worry about; you might only need to hire the coach a few hours a week!

CHAPTER 5:
COACHING SKILLS FOR LEADERS

"In research conducted over the past three years, we've found that leaders who have the best coaching skills have better business results."

— VP of Global Executive & Organizational Development at IBM

One method to reap the benefits of coaching is to train your current leaders in those skills. This involves hiring a trainer, ideally a genuinely certified coach, to provide a workshop, or a series of workshops, on the main coaching skill set. Those workshops typically cover building rapport, reading body language, active listening exercises and how to ask appropriate, powerful questions. Discussing the drawbacks for leaders is key, because leaders inherently have an agenda, and true coaching doesn't.

It's important to understand bias, and how to recognize deletions, distortions, exaggerations. This exercise comes from Coach and Coaching Skills Instructor John Hardwick, and it is as simple as finding a third-day newspaper article. This is an article that comes out on day three of a big story where there's no actual new news, but the media wants to keep reporting anyway. Typically, there are no new facts present. Most of the content is a speculation, an assertion, or inference. Coaches and Trainers bring those articles in and ask everyone: what's a deletion? What's a distortion? What's an exaggeration here? From that perspective, you can tell: it's everywhere.

When you hear things like that—deletions, distortions, exaggerations—from your employees, you have to pin them down and get a clear response. Otherwise, they're so emotional that no one can figure out what the challenge is, but you know it's there. Something's at the root.

LEVERAGING NEUROSCIENCE

Coaching that uses a neuroscience background or brain research places importance on creating balance in the brain—to move the client from an all-emotional approach to one that is balanced with the logical side. A great approach to shift an employee from too much emotion to a balanced state is to ask a question that requires calculation, such as "how long have you been feeling this way, or when did you first notice this concern...?"

THE DIFFICULT CONVERSATIONS

Delivering difficult conversations tends to be the biggest challenge for leaders. Technically, these conversations have nothing to do with coaching. A difficult conversation involves a message that they have to deliver, like "your behavior is interrupting the workplace." That's not coaching because coaching doesn't have an agenda. That's truly performance management. Coaching skills can help you with this discussion, but it's important to make the distinction. All leaders need to understand what's an appropriate coaching conversation, and what's an appropriate performance management conversation. They don't ever mix. They might open and close the same conversation, but they're two completely different things.

Once, in Kuala Lumpur, I was delivering training with my colleague Coach Ray Mera, of Australia. This coaching workshop was for an organization's top-fifty leaders and included a portion on delivering difficult conversations. We did what we always did: We broke them up into groups and had them start doing the demos. When we started listening in, I was in absolute shock—in all the demos, the person that was supposed to be getting fired thought they'd been promoted!

We immediately stopped them to figure out what was going on. We did a coaching session with the whole group, and that's how we realized we were implementing Western training techniques. Well, the Malaysian cultural values conflicted 100% with that; our training did not translate at all into delivering these difficult conversations. So, right then, we rewrote the entire procedure to be effective for Asia Pacific market.

What was fascinating was the amount of personal angst these people felt about delivering this news. No matter how much it was deserved, it was uncomfortable. Their culture is all about saving face. Using a coach approach with the group, we rewrote the training with more focus on the preparation. It became a lot more about what the leader could do to make sure that when the actual meeting happened, there was no question what it was about. They found a location that was very private. They made sure that the employee knew that this was a private meeting. They outlined step by step what they had to say, an actual script. Then they incorporated a way for the employee to save face, a plan how they were going to share it with the rest of the organization. If they were being fired, this person would have an opportunity to resign publicly.

It was different than I was used to. In the U.S., you've got to stick to the script; because of our litigious society, you can't say anything else. You can't say, "I'm sorry." You can't say anything extra. Then once you're done, (usually at that point the person wants nothing to do with you), you *can* offer support. This is where you can shift the 'performance management' side of management to the coach approach side of management. You can offer to partner with them to figure out what their next steps are, and that's where these skills come in.

Awareness of cultural norms and biases are important skills for leaders and coaches. The professional coach is trained to use the client's vocabulary, pace, and even tone to not only create rapport but to make it easier for the client. Less thinking and translating on the client's part allows for greater focus on their agenda. The style of the leader applying coaching skills should vary and adapt to the client and their cultural norms. These skills improve your ability to address and execute difficult conversations with more grace and sensitivity.

WHY LEADERS SHOULD USE COACHING SKILLS

Ever since the job market started dwindling, an unfortunate trend has emerged: the scarcity complex. For a lot of good reasons, people don't believe their jobs are safe—and finding a job is harder than ever. This leads to a few problems. First of all, employees are playing small. They don't want to be noticed because if one is noticed, they might be the next on the chopping block. Secondly, the managers dig in their heels because they're operating from fear as well. They become more and more controlling; they trust their own ideas more than their employees' ideas and insist everyone does it their way. Employees stop submitting their own ideas, and that hurts productivity. There will be a manager with ten employees, but only one person's brain is working.

And the vicious cycle continues. The managers become overworked and stressed out; they feel more and more resentful of their employees, who aren't stepping up, but to whom they've given every message *not* to step up. The employees, then, instead of taking risks and being innovative, just put their nose to the grindstone and work longer and longer hours to make themselves valuable.

Everyone in this situation is miserable.

> "To create a high-performance team, we must replace typical management activities like supervising, checking, monitoring, and controlling with new behaviors like coaching and communicating."
>
> RAY SMITH CEO, BELL-ATLANTIC

Coaching skills for the leaders in this organization will affect everyone below them in amazing ways. The manager learns to stop controlling everything; they start utilizing the gifts and talents of their employees to do what has to be done. They have requirements, of course; some things are just sent from above, and no one has a choice. But now they're asking their employees: How do you think we should do this? What are our options? Who should we bring in?

They start engaging the employees in the process. Then, once an employee submits an idea that's chosen, that employee takes more ownership of it. Why? They feel like they can take risks. They feel like someone's got their back. When it's okay to fail, your successes get noticeably more consistent. This can turn the company around; it allows them to use the output of all the employees, not just the leaders. There's more trust, and a culture of trust can outperform any other kind of leadership.

SCALABLE PEER COACHING

A program developed and used with success for peer coaching called Coaching in the Round, allows leaders to practice their coaching skills. Anyone, who has completed initial coach training can enroll based on their availability. Typically arranged using a two or three-month term, each person is assigned a coach and a client. All participants play both roles, each provides coaching, and each participates as a client. The objective is to participate in real coaching sessions with one another, to practice their skills, and the last five minutes of each session, the client gives feedback to the coach. My colleagues recommend several methods of feedback including *'Ask then tell,'* which involves the coach providing three things they believe went well in the session; the client also responds with three 'well done' observations. The coach then responds with one thing they would do differently, and the client responds with an opportunity for improvement as well. Another recommended peer feedback technique is to leverage Marshall Goldsmith's "peer coaching" video (see resources.)

The benefits of this peer feedback program include scalability. Follow a half-day workshop on coaching skills, with regular coaching practice and peer feedback before scheduling follow-up training. This allows development of questions by the leaders regarding challenging situations they have encountered in their practice. Depending on the organization's needs, it may be wise to introduce standard coaching procedures in the follow-up training and Q&A session. The peer-to-peer coaching is effective because leaders are exempted from situations that may reveal their own agenda. If a leader began practicing coaching skills immediately with employees but was then faced with a coaching topic from their employee that revealed a conflict with the manager's own agenda, the manager would naturally defend their own agenda. The beauty of peer practice circles is that a peer can just operate as the client.

Coaching Skills for Leaders is the most pervasive, and cheapest way to start a coaching culture in your organization. The challenge is, of course, maintaining that regular follow-up and including regular supervision to ensure effectiveness. Otherwise, it will be a complete waste of money, and resources, and time.

> "Xerox Corporation carried out several studies on coaching. They determined that in the absence of follow-up coaching to their training classes, 87% of the skills change brought about by the program was lost."
>
> -Business Wire

THE COACHING FOLLOW-UP

After any workshop, the follow-up with the coach is essential. The martial arts white belt can do all of the things the black belt can do, but the black belt has made them habitual. They've perfected each of those skills so masterfully that there's a significant distinction from the white belt. It's not what they can do—it's how they do it.

When your leaders are trained with internal coaching skills, they've got to keep learning from the master, a professional coach, if they want to make it a habit. The skills can apply to every level of leadership; usually, after working with the top brass, they want all their managers to have it—even leaders who aren't necessarily managers, but who are the go-to people in the organization. With so much peer coaching going on, this can be very effective. Some organizations elect to train their entire workforce in these skills.

The follow-up can be as simple as a workshop. Size is not a significant driver in providing a workshop. Workshops can be done with as many as fifty people, although the more attendees, the more facilitators you'll need. When everyone breaks up into groups practicing coaching, there's got to be enough knowledgeable coaches providing oversight and guidance. If the leadership team has completed a coaching skills workshop, those same leaders can share their experiences and help facilitate when a workshop with the rest of the staff is held. It comes full-circle.

Whether your company has ten people or 10,000 people, you can benefit from coaching skills. But if you want your investment to actually last, you have to do the follow-up.

THE SIMPLICITY OF COACHING

When implementing any new program, a pilot is always a good idea. As an organization, determine the goals you have for implementing the program. What are the key performance indicators you are hoping to influence? How are they performing today? Will this be the only intervention you'll be using? Or will this be part of a leadership development program—using mentoring and training as well as coaching? Can you attribute all of the improvements to the pilot? How will you measure your return on investment or expectation?

Implementing a coaching culture training, with all of its possibilities, can seem overwhelming. Regina Leeds - author of *One Year to an Organized Work Life* said, "Any chaos, is the result of an unmade decision." What are the decisions you need to make? Any ICF-Certified Coach with experience in building a coaching culture, in an environment similar to yours, can help get you started. A coaching culture can start with one workshop, one session. You don't have to know all the answers; Just like in the coaching conversation you'll create awareness, set goals, evaluate options, design actions and manage your accountability.

If one of the leaders enjoys the process of coaching enough, they might want to train to become a professional a coach themselves. Perhaps an HR person recommends that this is the cheapest way to increase your employee engagement. Coaching skills workshops may be offered for entire teams, as elective classes, or for one segment of your employee population. They've all been equally effective. It all depends on what works best for you.

"Investing in your people by delivering a good coaching program is a key component of a leader's development. It helps instill critical practices as participants begin to understand what good coaching looks like and how to bring it into play themselves."—Tech CU Chief Operating Officer Jeannine Jacobsen, as quoted in Coaching World Magazine, when interviewed about their organization building a coaching pilot.

Time and time again I've seen the internal grassroots groups reach out for coaching—a group of employees who care, who want their leaders to grow. For anyone who experiences coaching first hand, they want to bring it in. They want their managers to have it. They want their CEO's to have it. They want *you* to have it. They care about the company and their role in it—and they want to expand. Organizations such as Oracle and HP began internal coaching and coaching skills training for leaders through grassroots movements such as this. It provides a momentum and population of employees to ensure support of implementation. It is not uncommon in coaching program evaluations for individual contributors to recommend coaching and coaching skills training be offered to all leaders. This enthusiasm and support can help market your programs and ensure continuation after the pilot phase of the coaching project.

CHAPTER 6:
INTERNAL COACHING

Internal coaches are employed by the company they're coaching for. It can be a portion of their job, or it can be a full-time job. It can have very specific focus, or just be there for general well-being. The shoe company Zappos, at the time of this writing, has three internal coaches that are exclusively dedicated to the employees. Employees sign up for a three-month engagement, and they can be coached on anything. It could be life, can be work, relationship...it's there for their disposal.

The benefit to having a larger number of coaches trained and eventually certified is that it further broadens the coaching culture across the company and also allows for scalability to provide support for talent management programs or other specific efforts. Also, I believe the credibility is maintained at a high level when the coach can still speak the language of the business imperatives and is up to date on the concerns of their peers, not just as a coach, but as a fellow participant. (For this same reason, I do not advocate for the placement of coaches in the Human Resources department). It is important that the coaches get to practice their coaching regularly and have mentor coaching and supervision available to hone their skills.

THE ICF INTERNAL COACHING COMMUNITY OF PRACTICE (CoP)

The ICF has a wonderful Community of Practice for Internal Coaches that is open to all coaches who work internally. Research developments and best practices are regularly shared in meetings. I highly recommend any internal coach to take advantage of this resource.

Some organizations promote from within to create these internal coaching roles. One of my clients works in the heavy equipment industry. He has a phenomenal sales record, but because of a life change and sincere interest, he wants to be a coach for the sales people in his organization. As an expert in their department, with a proven track record and ample credibility, he's an ideal candidate to become a coach. His organization sent him to coaching school, as a path towards certification, and I'm working with him as his mentor coach. Every internal coach needs a mentor coach; it's one way to ensure they're practicing the competencies effectively. Whenever they face challenges within the organizational structure, or policies, or even with their own client calls, they have somebody that they can go to for support.

> ## THE MENTOR COACH
>
> A mentor coach provides both mentoring and coaching to a less experienced coach. Their role is to partner to develop the coach's skills, and ensure proficiency in the ICF's core competencies, as well as building their personal foundation. The personal foundation is an important aspect as unresolved issues can interfere with a coach's effectiveness with their clients. In the same way that a personal trainer should be fit, the coach should be a model for their clients. Finally, the mentor coach can help the coach with developing their practice. The ICF requires a minimum of ten hours with a mentor coach devoted to developing their skills and proficiency in the core competencies for ACC certification.

Some organizations hire an outside coach to become an internal coach and full-time employee. A typical coach job posting and description will require ICF certification which demonstrates coaching experience, training, and the mastery of a Coach Knowledge Assessment exam, as well as completing a coaching assessment (oral exam.)

However you choose to hire an internal coach, this is only an option if your company can afford the salary, payroll, taxes, and benefits for a dedicated coach. Once an organization reaches 30 employees participating in regular coaching, it may be more cost-effective to hire a half-time internal coach or train one of your current employees to take on that role half-time, than to work with an external one. However, there may be situations where supplementing with an external coach is still appropriate—such as sensitive performance management issues or scenarios where an external perspective is helpful.

INSIDE OR OUTSIDE?

Until about five years ago, the most common trend was to hire from the outside. This has been advantageous as the coach is already trained, and the coach comes in with a lot of experience. As a faculty member with Coach U, I see more and more companies sending their people to coach school for training. The advantage to that is they're already familiar with the company norms and culture, which can be a challenging fit for an outsider. There are some real advantages to having someone understand your culture and the way things work.

If you choose to train a current employee, that person must be well-respected by the workforce in their current role, whatever that role might be. It must be someone with a high degree of emotional intelligence, with the ability to read the political landscape. It has to be someone who isn't attached to their ideas because otherwise, they're going to be falling back into mentoring all the time. In their coach role, they will not be providing advice regardless of subject. They must also be comfortable in enabling others to achieve, rather than being the achiever themselves.

One challenge that is unique to the internal coach is when the company's standards of business conduct supersede the coaching code of ethics. For example, when the internal coach reviews the coaching agreement, with the client, it must be clarified. The code of ethics states that all our conversations are confidential (with few exceptions—see the code of ethics in resources), but if you violate the company's standards of business conduct, I am obligated to report you.

Another unique challenge to the internal coach is conflicting perspectives. They might be coaching different people who have multiple perspectives on the same problem, and that can be tense. If you're coaching the supervisor *and* the direct report, and one of them has information that the other one doesn't, you have to keep that knowledge to yourself—but balancing what you can and can't say gets tricky. Even if you can clearly see the breakdown in communication between the two, you can't make the connections for them. You can suggest they talk to each other, but that's about it.

The more masterful the coach, the less of a challenge this presents.

SURRENDERING EXPERTISE

A lot of the struggles that new internal coaches face are true for leaders learning coaching skills, too. Anyone transitioning from their current role to coach has a tough time refraining from judgment and advice. Before coaching, their whole life, their whole role, was to judge and give advice. This was the value add-on you provided in your non-coaching roles. Breaking this habit can be frustrating. My students are constantly battling this issue. A coach to a finance executive might ask: What's important to you with your money? How do you intend to use your money? They will *not*, however, suggest an instrument to use to track their money. Training an internal coach is about making sure they understand when to apply those skills, and when (if ever) it's appropriate to switch to a professional advisor role. This can be very confusing when they're first learning, and some personalities can't handle it. If you're someone who just loves to pontificate, you're going to be a horrible coach. Those new to coaching must embrace curiosity and not knowing as well as restraint.

As my fellow coaches kid, if you just have way too much knowledge to not share, you should be a consultant, not a coach. Coaching skills can serve you well as a consultant, but you'll be doing something inherently different. And if you need further incentive to refrain from advising, Coach Ed Nottingham makes an excellent point—"if you think it is easier to tell than to ask, remember that telling does not lead to behavioral change."

USING COACHING AS A TOOL

Internal coaching is a fixed expense; part of your payroll and your headcount. Sometimes that can be frustrating for a manager who needs more employees to accomplish a particular project; they see the internal coach as an impediment to that. Nevertheless, the internal coaches *have* to be part of the business. Don't shuffle them off to HR. Your coach is an asset, a part of the business that gets real work done. It needs to be taken seriously, like any other business tool. That's where you're going to get your biggest ROI.

Sometimes there can be conflicts of interest with an internal coach, especially if they're working with both a manager and an employee. A manager might approach the internal coach and ask him to work with Sam from Marketing because Sam had some problems in his last performance review. But the coach needs to clarify: this coaching is not corrective action; it's not an excuse for the manager to avoid their performance management duties. Everything the coach and Sam talk about is confidential. If the manager asks a week later about what happened in the coaching session, the coach can't talk about that. The manager has to speak with Sam himself.

The coach can also, at this point, set up a three-way conversation. This isn't necessarily a bad thing; as long as the manager respects the coach's boundaries, it can be helpful.

THE THREE-WAY AGREEMENT

The three-way agreement is the construction of a coaching agreement that defines the Leader's goals for the employee's coaching engagement, as well as the expectations of both the coach and the client. Included in this document is how the Leader will be informed on the progress of the engagement. This should include methods, frequency, and details. Because of the client confidentiality, the coach is not free to discuss the particulars of the sessions. Leaders frequently forget this and call the coach anyway. When this occurs, it is imperative that the coach limits the update, "The client is attending the sessions, and reports satisfaction. Please call the client to arrange for an update, I would be happy to attend if they would like me to join." This preserves the trust between the coach and client, the foundation of their relationship. If, or when, an update meeting happens (as arranged in the coaching agreement) the client leads the dialogue, not the coach.

PAYING FOR AN INTERNAL COACH

Long-term, the most sustainable coaching programs have the internal coaching component because the company has invested in it. They've made it part of their infrastructure; it's often even part of their business plan, especially if they have a focus within the company. A focus is necessary as it doesn't matter how many coaches you have—unless you're a tiny company—you probably can't coach *everybody*.

I was one person in a department of 10,000, and I was a full-time coach. My time was very dedicated regarding who I worked with. If other departments wanted to utilize my coaching skills, perhaps for a workshop of coaching skills for managers, they paid my department for my time (like rent.) This payment to my department helped relieve some of my expenses and allowed other departments to utilize a coach.

It usually takes a very insightful manager to implement this. These are the managers who can see the needs of the company over the needs of their individual department. The managers that have that kind of insight are usually the strongest; if they can spread the expense across multiple departments, that can be effective. If your department hires you out, they can earn back the money they're paying you. Plus, the higher the demand, the higher your rates can climb. The advantage to the leader who hosts the coach is control and accountability as well as setting the coach's focus. The advantage for the other departments that essentially rent the coach is access to a credible expert without having the carry the headcount or payroll.

MANAGEMENT OF CHANGE

In a previous role, my company was faced with significant downsizing due to offshoring work to a lower-cost location. Our affected workforce was in shock and dealing with the usual reactions of denial, anger and so forth. We needed a way to demonstrate our care for them, but also a method to place all of these individuals so that no one person would lose a job.

My brilliant leader at the time, Jim DuPree, had the insight that this shift was affecting many more than those who had been notified directly that their job would be changing. With his sponsorship, we embarked on offering a new methodology for our coaching using Laura Berman Fortgang's *Now What? 90 days to a New Life Direction*. As an authorized facilitator, I was able to offer Laura's 12-week program for any employee who wished to participate. This 12-week coaching program met weekly in groups, to cover the lessons in the book to receive coaching and create their Life Blueprint®.

The response was overwhelming; instead of offering one or two groups, we began with four and immediately followed the conclusion of the program with the two more offerings. The results from the surveys demonstrated that employees were even more engaged after their participation, including comments such as "The offering of this class made me feel like the company cared about me as a person." This program has been immensely popular and has been continually offered since.

COMBINING THE MODALITIES

EXTERNAL COACHES

LEADERS USING
COACHING
SKILLS

INTERNAL
COACHES

Often, when companies hire an internal coach, they'll also have an external coach (or a roster of external coaches) to cover the conflict of interests or confidentiality that might come up. Most Fortune 500 companies, for example, use an external coach roster for certain higher-ups. The dividing line is different in different companies: it might be C-suite (those who have C in their title, CEOs, CIOs, COOs), it could be directors and above. Some companies have as many as one thousand vice-presidents. For most of them, it is a title for their business cards that provides them access to see the CEOs of smaller companies. Not all of those one thousand VPs would need an external coach because not all of them are in the major leadership positions.

A combination of the modalities will provide the most flexibility and create the strongest coaching culture. A coaching leadership style will be the easiest on your leaders, the most attractive to millennials and solicit the most powerful ownership and innovation from your employees. Internal coaching is the most sustainable option for long-term growth and impact.

An excellent example of combining all three modalities to create a coaching culture is highlighted in a Press Release provided by the ICF — In 2016, the pharmaceutical company GlaxoSmithKline (GSK) won the ICF International Prism Award. Their coaching program employed all three modalities. GSK has roughly 100K employees. To provide coaching to ~5400 employees, they used 214 External Coaches, 1,085 Internal Coaches, and 16,500 Managers and Leaders trained in coaching skills.

Highlights of their program include: Coaching is available all employees at every level due to strong support from the current CEO and the CEO designate.

Even more impressive, the organization saw $66M USD return on their investment from this coaching initiative.

Their primary focus in developing the coaching program was to attract, develop and retain talent. This required establishing a Coaching Center of Excellence, standardizing coaching globally, by improving access, ensuring quality and efficiency and creatively containing costs. All coaching expenses were charged to the business units using the coach's services. *To read more about GSK's International Prism Award winning program, see resources.*

Now that you have a firm grasp of the modalities and how they can work together let's go through the Best Practices for key roles and functions in any coaching program.

CHAPTER 7:

BEST PRACTICES FOR KEY ROLES & FUNCTIONS

The key roles and functions involved in a coaching program follow:

- Human Resources (HR)
- Sponsors
- Stakeholders
- Coaches
- Clients

Additionally, you may have functions such as:

- A Coaching Program Manager
- A Coaching Community of Practice (CoP)
- A Coaching Center of Excellence (CoE)

It's important that all of these functions understand their roles and responsibilities for the program, but also what drives one another's motivation to support or implement the program.

First, I'll introduce a structure called a RASCI chart to help explain possible responsibilities across the key players and possible decisions for which they may be responsible. Then I'll follow with introductions of each of the key players, and finally a list of best practices for the players.

THE RASCI CHART

In business and project management, we often refer to the RASCI chart, an acronym for 'responsibility assignment matrix.' Each letter corresponds to roles in decision-making for a program or project.

The R stands for Responsible: This is the person (within a function) who has the duty and obligation to do the work. They're in charge of implementing the program.

The A is Accountable: They might not be running the program, but they're the 'neck that gets choked' if it's not done properly.

The C is the Consulted: This function consults with those who are responsible. They advise on the implementation. They are often affected by the program and therefore have a voice.

The S is Supporting: This function has a duty to help, but they're not necessarily running the overall program. They're helping implement the program or removing obstacles; like the busboys at the restaurant, you might not always see them, but without their work, the program wouldn't run.

The I is the Informed: These are the people who aren't a part of the program and who have no say or control over it but do need to be aware it's happening. For example, the lower level employees who don't work with the coach, but who know that their manager is in the coaching program.

A SAMPLE RASCI FOR A
COACHING PROGRAM

	HR	Sponsors	Stakeholders	Program Manager	Center of Excellence	Coaches	Clients
Source of funding for the program	I	R/A	I	S	I	I	I
Referring clients to the program	R	S	R/A	S	S	S	S
Measuring the Program and reporting results	S	A	I	R	S	S	I
Marketing the Program	R	S	R	A	S	R	S
Create Shared Operating Procedures	S	I	I	S	R/A	S	I
Facilitate Best Practices	S	I	I	S	R/A	S	I

THE KEY PLAYERS

HUMAN RESOURCES (HR)

Human Resources (HR), bless them, are often the ones wanting to implement coaching. They're the ones who got into the business world because they love people. Unfortunately, the businesses they work for are often only focused on executing top and bottom-line performance. They don't have the interest or the time to investigate new opportunities for employee engagement. Which means that over the years, the HR profession evolved in a significant, though not necessarily beneficial, direction.

In the early '90s, HR was the employee advocate. They looked out for how to develop people, how to manage talent, how to hold on to assets, and more. Now, it's more about policy and legal protection for the company, especially in the US.

There's a lot of dollars and headcount work that happens in the upper levels of HR. Very few people enter HR to become a policy and numbers person, but that's what happens. They bring coaching in because they intuitively know the difference it can make. The data's there to support that, but the overall success will depend entirely on the receptivity of the organization.

THE SPONSORS

When it comes to implementing coaching, the first key role is the sponsor—traditionally the leader who funds the program. This the most obvious option, of course, is the person who's in charge of the company or department that's implementing the program. But in some organizations, cross-pollination can happen: one department has a little extra in the funds this year, and they owe you a favor. Wherever the funds come from, one person—and only one—needs to be accountable. You can't have two kings (or queens), of the kingdom. There's nothing wrong with having a bigger team in charge of overseeing or implementing the program, but there should only be one person the program ultimately reports to.

THE STAKEHOLDERS

The stakeholders might not be funding the project, but they all get a vote. They all have an influence on the coaching program because the program is in their department or organization. One of these stakeholders might also be HR; HR is almost always an influencer when it comes to any kind of human capital or human development program. They tend to be the ones who enlighten the people busy working on costs and sales, who might not have time to look up and notice the state of their people.

There's also an audience of stakeholders that I would call self-refer. This is often the base of a grassroots movement: enlightened and motivated to make a change. They pursue opportunities to develop and learn. If organizations make room for those people, they can make dramatic changes—including bringing on a coaching pilot program! This may also be the base of your Coaching Community of Practice (CoP).

COACHABILITY

Janice Flor said, "You can't push a parked car." Whether you're talking about an individual or an organization, they have to be coachable. That's the willingness to question their beliefs, and it's essential for coaching to succeed. In April 2009, an initial study was conducted with the ICF's Internal Coaching Community of Practice (CoP), then known as a special interest group (SiG). It revealed "the willingness to question one's beliefs' was the number-one factor determining 'coachability.' " (See Coaching World July 2009). If a company believes that their current employee engagement program is adequate, trying to introduce coaching will be a struggle. They'll be too skeptical. On the other hand, if they're willing to experiment and take a test drive, all of the data out there shows the return on investment.

THE COACHES

The coaches are those who are trained in coaching skills and on their way to certification, if not already certified. (ICF credentialed coaches come in three levels of mastery based on their hours of training, hours of coaching performed and proficiency in the coaching competencies) They perform the duties of coaching the individual clients and reporting their coaching hours.

THE CLIENTS

The final key player in the whole coaching program are the clients: Those who actually receive coaching. They are truly the best way to measure the success of the program. With before and after surveys, you can monitor whether they enjoyed being coached, what it did for them, and what, in their view, they were able to accomplish because of it. If they were able to get a promotion, to stick with a job they hadn't planned on, or develop a new packaging technique, you have right there the benefits of the program in a measurable form. Use their experience as the basis for measurement, then expand from there.

ADDITIONAL FUNCTIONS

There are three additional functions, that may be shared or have some overlap, that can bring formality to your program and enhance your results:

COACHING PROGRAM MANAGER

A coaching program manager may be a coach, or a project manager but is responsible for driving the implementation of the program, ensuring standards are being met, reporting progress to sponsors, and spreading news of results across the organization. This may be a portion of a role once the program is up and running, but is essentially a different skill set than that of a coach.

COMMUNITY OF PRACTICE (CoP)

This is the collection of those interested in the practice of coaching. The membership may include internal coaches, managers practicing coaching skills, external coaches, those interested in using coaching skills for mentoring, or other roles that can benefit. Typically, the community is open for all who are interested. The community may have an online presence to share tips and tools, and also meet regularly to discuss topics in coaching.

CENTER OF EXCELLENCE (CoE)

A center of excellence is one that is interested in promoting the standards, and profession of the craft of coaching. It may overlap some with CoP, but has distinct responsibilities in defining standard documentation and procedures, policies for dealing with new emerging issues and is more dedicated to the profession.

COLLABORATING

Often, each of these key players has their own motivations and measures that they see as an indicator of success. The players may not have clear insights into one another's needs; sometimes, in matrixed organizations, they may even have conflicting goals. It's important that whatever modality (internal, external or leaders with coaching skills) you use, try to look at it from the well-rounded approach of all the needs and people involved. It is essential that the key players co-create a collective set of goals for the program and what constitutes success.

The internal coach may be able to glean collective insights from the actual sessions that apply to the organization as a whole. They see the new awareness, the productivity, and the actions that are taken by their clients, thanks to coaching. But that may take a while for the cumulative effect to be noticed by the higher-level stakeholders. The executives, on the other hand, they're looking at the overall growth. They're looking at those KPIs almost exclusively, without anecdotal information. An HR person's goal is often for things to run smoothly. They want to see this implemented well, they want to manage the risks. Their reputation might be on the line, but the internal coach won't necessarily be aware of that—or vice versa.

Without seeking all of these perspectives, you might not be able to report the results in a manner that is attractive to the sponsor. The internal coach has all the anecdotal information, but they have to keep it all confidential. That doesn't do anything for the sponsor, who needs to know the results.

The executives are often the key to this proof of concept. Not only do they need to have experience getting coached, but they also need to know the perspectives of all the players to get behind the program. As a consultant, I always advocate for the executives to experience coaching first before we do anything else. If they don't know what it's like, there's no way that they can make an educated decision on what it could be like for their lower-level employees.

Then again, if the executives are simply enjoying the perks of having an external coach, they often just take it for granted that this is *their* development. They fail to translate their experience to something that would benefit all of the lower levels. They figure, "Well when I make a good decision, it's worth millions of dollars. When they make a good decision, it's worth 15 minutes." But if they can see the ROI, if they can see the perspectives of all these players, they'll see that coaching is the lever that can make a difference with their employees, and with their bottom line.

BEST PRACTICES

Once you bring on the coaching, there are a few important things to consider:

WHERE COACHES WILL SIT

- Don't make an actual coaching department
- Do create a coaching center of expertise and/or a community of practice

When coaches are removed from the business, they are considered less credible and trusted due to their distance. They're not involved in the business side of things, so when push comes to shove and the company has to cut costs, they cut the whole department! They weren't able to see their value, because they were so separate.

Whether internal or external, coaches need to sit in on the business side of things and understand what's happening. Sometimes, HR can live in its own little bubble. They don't understand the dynamic challenges that are happening in the actual workforce; don't let that rub off on your coaches.

THE COACH

COACHING HOURS

Coaches I interviewed spent anywhere from 8 to 30 hours coaching each week. Depending on the other responsibilities of your coaches, and whether they have coaching as a part of their role versus their entire role, the number of clients they can support varies.

Most agree that 45-90 minute sessions are ideal. Coaches were split on bi-weekly or monthly meetings. Seeing greater than six clients in a day was challenging for focus. Coaches definitely need breaks between clients for the purposes of mentally switching gears, taking notes and breathing room.

Do not believe that your coach has forty hours a week to coach. They don't. They still have to go to staff meetings, do required corporate training, answer emails—all the challenges that you battle with, they battle with, too.

COACHING NOTES

Coaches *should* keep their coaching notes separate from their business notes. They need to be in a separate file in a locked space. Then, when they're done with that client, they need to shred those notes. If organizations become involved in lawsuits, the coaches' notebooks are discoverable. Protect that confidentiality: keep the notes separate, and destroy them when they're no longer relevant.

HOW TO USE THE COACH

There's a million and one ways coaches can improve your ROI. Sometimes, it's as simple as helping people acclimate more quickly to a new job, a new level, or a new company. When a coach is present in the business, they can help with reducing costs, promoting innovation or increasing sales. The applications are too many to list, but here are a few.

GROUP WORK

Coach work can be applied in group settings; such as working with a sales force, examining the routine of the sales people. How often are you doing cold calls? How often are you following up on those calls? They get into the details of the company's day-to-day; they create awareness. This doesn't mean consulting; they're utilizing the knowledge a company has and holding them accountable. For example, the coach may have been informed that the average customer buys on the fourth contact. If you give up on the first one, then you probably won't close that deal. The coach can therefore be present and actually ask the salesperson, "How often do you go back four times?"

NEW HIRES

Probably one of the most effective applications I've seen for coaching is when a company uses it for new hires. Within a year, that new employee has made up their mind whether they are going to stay. Those first few months are critical in terms of getting to know the company and feeling at home. Again, we go back to those Q12 questions: "Do I feel like I belong? "Do I know what's expected of me? Do I have a friend here at work?"

Coaching gives new employees a safe place to ask the questions that they want to ask, but that they anticipate might leave a sour taste in the mouth of whoever's training them, like questions about vacation. This type of early intervention program can be especially significant for millennials, who are relationship-driven. They want to have someone that they can go to. Anybody who's a veteran in the company is going to have more experience than the new hire, but some of those questions might make them a little uncomfortable—they're about policy as opposed to culture, and the veteran doesn't want to answer incorrectly.

Once, I was mentoring a new hire who lived in a different city than I did. She had come from the university where I was a mentor in the business school, so I was trying to help her out with some questions as she started work. She should have asked her manager, but she was afraid to; I asked her about her job description, but she didn't know what a job description was!

Sometimes, just having that mentor or a coach to disclose what should have happened, to let you in on the ins and outs, is enough to help someone get settled.

Now that we've covered the options and key players required to make your program run, as well as a few best practices, we'll dive into how to implement your program using your chosen modalities.

PART IV: THE HOW

CHAPTER 8:
DESIGNING & MEASURING YOUR COACHING PROGRAM

"Employers are shocked at how high their ROI numbers are for coaching. He recalls a large employer in the hospitality industry saved between $30 million and $60 million by coaching its top 200 executives."

—ACCENTURE, ALASTAIR ROBERTSON,
Manager of worldwide leadership development

DESIGNING WITH THE END RESULT IN MIND

In Stephen Covey's classic, *The 7 Habits of Highly Effective People*, Covey states habit two as 'begin with the end in mind." This principle holds true for designing effective coaching programs.

Consider the following:
- What is your current situation?
- What is the goal of the organization?
- What are the stated objectives that will reach that goal?
- What are the strategies to achieve the stated objectives?

- How will we measure the success of those strategies?
- When will we complete the implementation of those strategies?

This order and outline for goal attainment is not uncommon, but knowing where your coaching program fits within this outline is important. Is it a goal to create a coaching culture? Or is a coaching culture a strategy to improve employee engagement?

The program should be designed to improve the goals and the key performance indicators (KPIs) of the organization, such as financial performance, employee engagement, manager effectiveness, or retaining women in executive positions.

To effectively attribute improvements in any area, regardless of goal, the goals must be stated with the baselines measured.

In this chapter, we'll review several designs and methods for measurement.

KEY PERFORMANCE INDICATORS (KPIs)

Aspirations and threats are two areas that often drive an organization and create the metrics that are reviewed on a regular basis. In coaching, these metrics are referred to as the Key Performance Indicators (KPIs). If an organization can identify these KPIs they wish to influence, they have completed the first step for a successful coaching implementation.

The baselines for the KPIs and their methods of measurement must be identified. For example, if you wish to improve attrition, what is the current attrition rate? If you would like to improve innovation, how do you measure innovation? Perhaps it is patent applications or proposals to management. If you wish to improve productivity, how do you measure it today?

Once the KPIs and the methods of measurement have been established and agreed upon (please document this) then you are ready to apply your coaching program. Ideally, your coaching program is the only intervention (improvement plan strategy) applied to these specific KPIs. As this is the only way to discreetly attribute the success to the coaching program measures.

Beyond Emancipation (B:E), a non-profit serving emancipated foster youth in the Oakland, California area, used a creative approach to their KPIs that supported their clients. An honorable mention International Prism Award winner in 2016, B:E set out to improve the key success factors for their clients, rather than traditional measures in organizations such as funding, staff turnover, or communications.

B:E specifically identified:

- Safe and secure housing for clients
- Post-secondary education persistence and completion
- Career development training completion
- Job placement and retention
- Increased self-advocacy skills

By focusing on these KPIs in their coaching culture, B:E secured a retention outcome almost twice as high as those for foster youth in California community colleges overall, in addition to other improvements.

"We owe it to our young people to do things differently," adds B.E's Executive Director, Kate Durham. "That's the argument for building a coaching culture."

The B:E story shows what can be accomplished when organizations focus their coaching programs on the most important metrics to the business. To read more about B:E's case study and organizational snapshot, go to https://coachfederation.org/files/FileDownloads/Case-Study_Emancipation.pdf

SURVEYS

Surveys are an excellent way to determine improvement in a process or organizational progress towards a goal. In the following section, we'll cover several designs for surveys.

GOAL IMPROVEMENT

As with organizational goals, and KPIs, individual coaching should also be approached with the end in mind.

Introducing the Radar Chart to track Client's Goals and Progress

The first session agenda with a coach has several items. These can be done in any order, but they need to happen before "coaching" begins.

Agenda items include:

- Reviewing the coaching agreement (a contract)
- Getting to know one another
- Discussing the client's goals for the engagement (the entire duration of the time the coach and client work together)
- Answering any questions the client has about the process.

The goals discussion helps establish the plans for the engagement. The discussion must also include where the client is today in relation to those goals. This establishes a baseline for future measurements of the client's progress. The tool I created to help visualize these baselines of the client's multiple goals is a radar chart. (see figure below) This can also be used to report the average progress per participant by summarizing progress at an amalgam level. (see blue box in diagram)

A radar chart looks like a spider web; it has multiple spokes, and each spoke represents a goal. I usually start with three and establish clear ways to measure those goals. Then, if we have more time, we'll even do a breakdown structure for each of them.

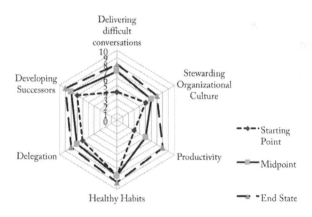

Engagement goals show an average increase of 19 points per participant

Set the baseline. Then, at three months, re-measure. Look at the goals from the last nine sessions, see how things have improved, and decide if they want to shift to another target area or keep going.

Sometimes that first measurement is a big wake-up

call because they realize they've been wasting their sessions, by not applying their goals as topics for the sessions.

Then, it's the coach's job to hold them accountable to that. If in the next session they bring up another topic that doesn't have to do with their stated goals, the coach should challenge them, "When we first started the engagement, we said *this* is important, and you wanted to work on *these* things. Do you still want to work on this new thing, or do you want to work on _____??"

With my clients, if they evade it for too long, I'm probably going to get in their face about it. I'm going to push them to discover whether they're actively avoiding it for a reason. Sometimes they know they're self-sabotaging—if you never try, failing doesn't hurt so much.

I had an executive who valued family time very highly. One of his rules for himself was that: "I always fly home. I don't stay the night to take the morning flight." But when we dug into it, he realized that he worked late so many nights, he almost always missed dinner with his family. So, what was the point of his grand always-fly-home rule if he didn't actually see them?

We put a measurement in place: every morning he reported to his admin, who kept track of whether he had dinner with his family or not. That was one of the spokes on his wheel—to maintain that. For him, that was the definition of balance. He could work 12 hours, but as long as he was home for dinner, that was all that counted because that was his quality time.

In the following example, a client has stated the goal of improving executive presence. The components of executive presence are then separated and evaluated as individual goals, each with its own baseline or starting point (these become the spokes of the radar chart). Then midway through the engagement, similar to conducting a pulse survey, another evaluation is conducted between the coach and client, and finally, at the end of the engagement, the evaluation is performed again.

Goals: Executive Presence

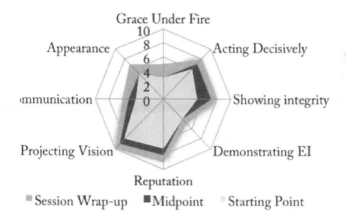

GOAL-ATTAINMENT & CONFIDENCE-SCALING

Leveraged from a similar instrument in the counseling industry, goal-attainment and confidence scales measure the organizational or individual confidence in meeting a goal. This process asks that participants imagine being beyond the end date of their goals, such as the date of a desired marathon, or the implementation date of a software program. The individual is then asked to project on a scale of 1-10 their confidence level in having achieved that goal, and if not, what got in the way. So, a participant may offer their confidence level at only a 7 in having run the marathon. When asked why not a 10, they may offer reasons such as overtraining led to injury, due to not having a proper training base. Their confidence level for the software may only have been a 6, due to political infighting and lack of clear ownership in decision-making. These projections for less than 100% confidence in goal-achievement, were proven to be highly accurate in predicting reasons and helpful in risk-planning.

INTERNAL SURVEYS & PULSE SURVEYS

If you do a workshop with just the leadership team, and you want to evaluate whether it's effective enough to expand to include all of the managers, you'll want to do a survey of the employees of that executive team. Do they have any observations about their leader? Have they noticed any differences? That's going to be the real measure of success. Those kinds of things anecdotally make a huge difference in the company. If you have ten people say "I felt freer to submit my ideas and they were actually heard," well, those could be the ten breakthrough ideas for the company.

The survey should also tie back to the goals and KPIs of the program. If the intention was to reduce attrition, or build confidence in new hires, be sure the survey tracks the progress.

A good survey should also, of course, check in with the actual leaders getting trained. Specifically look for whether the leader has greater confidence in their employees, whether they notice their coaching skills affecting their bottom line because that's what's going to demonstrate to everyone involved whether this program is worth it.

PULSE ASSESSMENT

As you continue with your program, don't forget to assess your progress along the way. Start with a quick pulse survey; this isn't a grand formal assessment, it's just a quick survey to check in with the participants. Ask them how the process is working, and whether they're finding it effective. If so, how? If not, why not?

NET PROMOTER SCORE

Frequently, coaching can discover connections and solutions you'd never expect. How much is your company's revenue affected by the personality of you CEO, for instance?

A popular measure is the Net Promoter Score. That's a benchmark for how happy customers are with your service. Would they recommend it to their friends? That's the leading indicator. Many times, the perception is that coaching might be able to change your team's human behavior, but it doesn't always actually affect that key performance indicator of the Net Promoter Score.

A colleague recalled working with an executive who was basically all numbers. He was entirely focused on the bottom line; he was good at his job and did a lot of great work, but he never walked around and asked how your weekend was. He never took his manager out to lunch to talk about things. Once he started getting coached, guess what?

His bottom line moved up.

Why? First of all, when you build relationships, you build trust. Whenever trust grows, there's a deeper desire to fulfill commitments. Secondly, just by walking around and saying good morning, chatting and building relationships, he's probably learning a lot about indirect influences. These might not be direct factors that influence the score immediately, but the little things add up. It wasn't as if he had discovered some secret problem that was delaying shipment; then again, he might have discovered how his employees enjoyed their shifts. He might have found a way to get people a better lunch break, or a more sustainable schedule. Those things affect the numbers.

Anything that increases employee engagement is going to be better for the customer in the long run.

NET PROMOTER SCORE

Net Promoter Score Definition: The Net Promoter Score is an index ranging from -100 to 100 that measures the willingness of customers to recommend a company's products or services to others. It is used as a proxy for gauging the customer's overall satisfaction with a company's product or service and the customer's loyalty to the brand.

Net Promoter Score Calculation Customers are surveyed on one single question. They are asked to rate on an 11-point scale the likelihood of recommending the company or brand to a friend or colleague. *"On a scale of 0 to 10, how likely are you to recommend this company's product or service to a friend or a colleague?"* Based on their rating, customers are then classified into 3 categories: detractors, passives, and promoters.

source: Medallia.com

GALLUP'S Q12

To find out whether your employee engagement rate does need work, or to see what kind of difference coaching made, you need a way to measure it. The quickest and easiest way to do this, if you don't currently have an employee survey, is the Q-12. That's the specific set of twelve questions to ask all your employees I mentioned before; you measure engagement from the feedback. These questions are all about connecting the employee's day-to-day work with the company's objectives.

Gallup's Q12 has been used for over 30 years in measuring engagement, (see introduction) with millions of participants. Visit http://www.gallup.com/services/190118/engaged-workplace.aspx to learn more.

COACHING WITH ROI

Created by the Bloom Coaching Institute, a measurement program to help coaches promote the accomplishments of their work. Lisa Ann Edwards shares "It's designed for one-on-one coaching engagements but can be used for team coaching and the collective results of small groups of clients as well." The evaluation method is designed with a monetary benefit focus. Created by an executive coach with an HR background as well as workforce analytics it:

- Begins and ends with the sales process in mind
- Includes a focus on behavior improvement
- Uses three levers of success (coachee characteristics, coaching solution and environment)

The goal is for the coach to be able to calculate the ROI, capturing data from the coaching client, within one coaching session; talk about the value of their work in monetary terms, documenting their success stories backed by evidence and data, including monetary value and ROI. www.BloomCoachingInstitute.com

THE KIRKPATRICK + PHILLIPS MODEL

KIRKPATRICK

Commonly used by training providers and created by Dr. Don Kirkpatrick in the 1950s, the model is applied before, during and after training to both maximize and demonstrate training's value to the organization.

- Level 1: Reaction- The degree to which participants find the training favorable, engaging and relevant to their jobs
- Level 2: Learning- The degree to which participants acquire the intended knowledge, skills, attitude, confidence and commitment based on their participation in the training
- Level 3: Behavior- The degree to which participants apply what they learned during training when they are back on the job
- Level 4: Results- The degree to which targeted outcomes occur as a result of the training and the support and accountability package

ADDING THE PHILLIPS' ROI

In the book *Measuring the Success of Coaching*, Phillips, Phillips & Edwards add a fifth dimension the Kirkpatrick model, Return on Investment (ROI.) Traditionally, this is expressed as a Benefits to Costs ratio, the monetary benefits divided by the costs. With coaching or training programs, a slight modification is made to this formula: the monetary benefits subtract the costs and then are divided by the costs, multiplied by 100 to reach a coaching ROI.

$$\frac{\text{Monetary Benefits} - \text{Investments}}{\text{Investments}} \times 100 = \text{ROI}$$

RETURN ON EXPECTATION

There are a lot of organizations that understand intuitively that coaching is beneficial, just like mentoring is beneficial. In those companies, we save a lot of time because we don't need to financially measure and prove every single point of growth; they expect growth and grow even more because of it. (We also save time in not arguing about whose number is right and how it was measured.)

With these organizations, we are satisfied with the return on expectation (ROE). We hypothesize that adding a coaching program to onboard new employees to help them acclimate to the new company will boost retention. We measure the attrition rates before and after implementing a coaching program to gauge results. We are satisfied with a reduction in attrition of new hires. This method of ROE can be applied to any goal or strategy coaching can address.

So many companies don't know those numbers. One of the aspects of the International Prism Award is ROI or ROE, and in some of the most effective, promising stories, people either don't report the numbers (ROI) because they're a privately-owned company, or they simply have no idea what those numbers are. Even Fortune 500 companies often don't know the actual costs associated with recruiting, interviewing, hiring and training new employees. Even if they cut their turnover rate in half, they couldn't tell you how much money it saved them!

How long do you wait for results? It depends on the metric you hope to affect. With individual improvement, our recommended timeframe is usually based on the level of the employee we're working with. If they don't have management responsibilities, it could be from three to six months; for a manager, it might be six months to a year; for an executive, it's a minimum of one year. A pulse survey can quickly assess the progress you've made, whether it's more or less than you were hoping, and how much further you have to go.

USING ICF'S PRISM CRITERIA

The ICF uses four main criteria in measuring the effectiveness of a coaching program for the International Prism Award.

- STANDARDS
- STRATEGY
- SUSTAINABILITY
- IMPACT

STANDARDS

The standards cover the professional standards of the program such as training and certifications of the individuals practicing coaching, the use of contracts or formal coaching agreements with the clients. Industry excellence such as mentoring for coaches and supervision of practice, and best practices including adopting the coaching code of ethics and confidentiality, and finally a strong understanding of the use and benefits of coaching over other modalities such as training, mentoring or consulting.

STRATEGY

This criterion demonstrates how the goals, values, and needs of the organization or individual are being addressed through coaching. The coaching is adaptable and evolves to client needs. It also proves to be a fundamental element to the success of the individual or organization.

SUSTAINABILITY

Demonstrates that the organization's commitment to the process and practice of coaching is now embedded with lifestyle, identity or culture of the company (or individual) and plans exist to develop further applications of coaching as a preferred long-term solution. Finally, the character of the persons or organization has changed due to coaching.

IMPACT

Measurable details underscoring value, influence or effectiveness of the coaching are present. Either KPIs, other metrics or evaluations show improvement due to coaching. Testimonials explain breadth and depth of the coaching impact and participants personally validate their observations of personal engagement or well-being improving due to the intervention of coaching. Finally, a return on the expected results of the program, from projected hypothesis, goal attainment or KPIs. And if possible, a financial measure of impact demonstrating the return on the investment made.

You can and should expect a significant ROE/ROI. When properly planned, the investment of coaching turns into more and happier customers, more revenue, improved employee-retention, lowered expenses, and more profit. By tracking the baseline of your key performance indicators before a coaching intervention, and then monitoring their progress towards your targets, during and after the coaching engagement, you'll recognize your returns.

CHAPTER 9:
IMPLEMENTING EXTERNAL COACHING

When searching for an external coach, the first step is to make sure that the body of coaches you're choosing from are credentialed. The International Coaching Federation (ICF,) is the largest, most recognized governing body when it comes to coaching. (The Center for Credentialing and Education also offers a Board-Certified Coach (BCC) Credential.) The ICF offers accreditation to qualified training programs, and awards credentials to the individual coaches. They have a database where you can search for coaches that have certain specialties or geographies; you can even submit a request for a proposal based on your specific needs. www.coachfederation.org

Credentials mean predictable levels concerning the standards and ethics that the coach will use, and the core competencies they're practicing. There are a lot of practitioners out there who call themselves coaches but have nothing to do with true coaching. They're actually practicing consulting or mentoring; those aren't necessarily bad things, of course, but you want to make sure that you fully understand what you're getting when you hire someone called a 'coach.'

If a company is interested in acting as their own talent broker for coaching talent, it can be an up to a six-month process to narrow down the responses, do the interviews with the coaches, and then do the follow-up and the selection process. (Also, the company may have vendor-approval processes, non-disclosure agreement, etc.) It may go more quickly, depending on the volume of coaches that you need. There are a number of talent brokers and other groups acting as executive coaching firms; they have considerable experience providing rosters of coaches to clients to choose from. Like any talent broker, they will take a fee and cost you, the client, more money; however, they will also do the work of recruiting coaches, vetting them, securing their references, ensuring their credentials are valid, etc.

You also only have to pay one bill, because you'll pay the brokerage house, not the individual coaches. If you decide to do the broker work in-house, that means that you'll do all the validation. You'll have to maintain a roster of coaches, and you'll have to set up all of those coaches as approved vendors.

If you *don't* go through a broker, at the very least go onto the ICF website to search the name of your potential coach. A quick search can pull up their whole profile (including credentials) in less than a minute.

If you're focusing on external coaches solely for one or a couple of the C-Suite, then it might be in your best interest to do the brokerage yourself. If you're looking to hire the equivalent of a whole department, it might be more beneficial to go through a brokerage. Ensure the client/employee has the opportunity to review the profiles of a wide array of coaches and make their own selection; fit is one of the most the important criteria for a successful coaching engagement.

I've also seen it the other way around: a pool of coaches will meet the entire group of coachees, and the *coaches* get together to suggest who they think they would fit with. That is a little bit unusual, but it can be effective.

A COACH FOR YOUR COACHING

No matter how much preparation you do for your program, it's always a good idea to have some consulting hours from an experienced coach to arrange or review your coaching project plan. I regularly do this in my own practice; I'm brought in to assess whether any given program has the right number of coaches for the right number of employees, that they're giving themselves enough time to be successful, and to help them establish a measurement of success.

A consultant can help you focus, determine the key performance indicator baselines, and even do initial interviews of the participants to determine which coaches are most appropriate. This investment in a consultant will save you money in the long run; you don't want to hire coaches who aren't a good fit, don't have the proper organizational coaching experience, or experience setting up programs of the size and nature you're seeking. Finally, a consultant can ensure the investment of your time and money too, and solves the right problem or can fulfill the opportunities you seek.

A lot of people who are less experienced with coaching might just try to implement a program without getting the stakeholders to experience coaching; or they might completely forget about the modality of training leaders with coaching skills, which could have just as much of an impact as the internal program that they're designing.

Once leaders have had the experience of coaching, and they understand the benefits, they can be much more effective in contributing to the design of the program. A consultant's experience will ensure that you design your coaching experiment in the best way possible.

IMPLEMENTING A PROGRAM

Once you've found your coach, there are a lot of things to consider as you get started. First of all, how long will your pilot program last? This will vary based on the organizational hierarchy levels of the clients. The following numbers are averages, not guidelines, and you should set your coaching engagements to be the estimated length needed to achieve the client's goals. Coaching agreements can always be renewed if the client feels they need a longer engagement. For executives, external coaching typically lasts a year to eighteen months. Managers average nine months, and for individual contributors, it's usually about six months. This will all depend on the frequency that the coach and the client meet, and the scope of their work—which should be established early on.

It's important to be open-minded as you develop your goals for this program; sometimes the problem you *think* needs solving isn't the actual issue. An external coach can bring in some serious insight as to what your actual problems are. Work with them to decide on the population you'll be targeting, the frequency of coaching, the method of meeting, and of course the system of measurement for your goals. You'll have to balance all this with your company's schedule and budget, but usually the coach can help you develop something that works for everyone.

Set some goals for the duration of the engagement.

If you'll be working with a coach for a year, what do you want to accomplish by the end of that year? Set a baseline for that as you begin. If you plan to work on executive presence, where are you *today* in your executive presence? Then, break down the gap between your goal and reality. Sometimes coaches start by observing the clients in meetings and creating some awareness of that baseline. They'll notice your habits, habits you might have unaware of, and review them with you. They might even interview your direct reports or peers. At my own company, we do something called the 360. The 360 is a survey that goes to the manager, the employees, the peers, the customers, etc.—and then comes back as a roughly 45-page report to assess where you're at. Sometimes an executive discovers that they're weak in a particular area, like external market awareness. They're so internally focused that they have no idea what their peers in the marketplace are doing. The 360 will recognize that gap so you can set goals for your coaching engagement and get you started on improving that skill.

PAIRING YOUR EXTERNAL AND INTERNAL COACHES

If, in the course of your coaching program, you decide to bring on internal as well as external coaches, don't forget to put those two parties in communication. Often, there's a formal separation, wherein the externals and internals don't talk to each other. They may not even know the other exists. There's absolutely no advantage to that, but it does happen. The external coaches are focused on the higher-level leaders, and the internal coaches are focused on lower levels.

If the external coaches are all working with the C-suite on preparedness for a new market category, that's going to affect those lower ranks. If the external and internal coaches are in contact, they don't have to disclose any details, but they can point one another in the right direction.

Similarly, connecting with each other about various observations and trends can help the external coaches get familiar with the company culture. Something that an external coach might think is a strange, isolated behavior may be part of the company culture, and he may not know it.

Other collaborative efforts could include: building a center of excellence, showcasing best practices and creating shared operating procedures as well as measuring the collective results of the program.

When referring to our modality of leaders using coaching skills—the combination of internal and external coaches as instructors may provide the richest experience. They can also provide follow-up training and supervision.

SITUATIONAL COACHING

As a coach works with you to develop the program, they may start from a place of situational coaching. One ICF-accredited school, Coach U, focusing on corporate coaching, trains their coaches on the ten most common kinds of client types, and the problems or issues that are most common for each type. There's the CEO, the entrepreneur, the professional, the artist, the academic, and so on. Coaches are trained in the common problems that each of these people faces. For example, it's very common for a CEO to feel like there's nobody they can trust.

They have to be careful who they reveal information to. The entrepreneur, on the other hand, commonly feels like they have to do everything. They answer the phones, they knock on doors for new business, *and* they're trying to innovate. A coach can help them concentrate on what they need to hire the right people and delegate accordingly.

All coaches try to figure out the baseline of where you are today. If you need to buff up your financial skills, where are you now? Can you read a financial statement? Can you look at a balance sheet? Do you feel confident in asking questions during a financial review? The coach may not have experience in finance, but they can help you create an awareness of what you need to improve.

An absolute requirement for every coaching engagement is a coaching *agreement*. This is basically a list of expectations for what the client is going to do, what the coach is going to do, and what will happen if those expectations aren't met. The agreement establishes a reliable exit plan if one or more parties are unhappy with how things are going.

Sometimes, the coach and the client just aren't a good match. The client might just stop showing up for sessions, rather than speak up about what's not working for them. A survey can spot those issues. Other times, clients just might not be ready for coaching. If they're not willing to look at themselves and actually discover what's inhibiting their success, no coach is going to be able to get through. A survey can catch that, too. Other times, the organization is asking them to do something that's outside their value set; they start to feel resentful about this, and they see themselves as selling out if they start complying.

In any of those instances, it's in the best interests of the coach *and* the client to sit down and ask if things are working. If not, why not? What could you do differently? Maybe the coach refers them to someone else; maybe we reorient the whole program.

I have a good friend, a brilliant scientist who went through coaching at the same time I did, as part of a talent management program early in our careers. He didn't care for it; he just figured it wasn't for him. But later, when he began working with me, he started to enjoy it; that was a reflection of having a coach he knew and trusted, which is important.

I always ask my clients what, exactly, they'd prefer me to do when they get behind on their goals. Do they want me to be encouraging and positive because everybody in their life is micromanaging them? Or do they really *need* at least one person to be micromanaging them, and that becomes my role as I hold them accountable? There are so many things that can get in the way, so it's important that the coach and the client have that trusted relationship. That's the only way they can have that discussion; if they don't ever do that, then the whole thing is a waste of time.

COACHING SCHOOLS AS A SOURCE FOR COACHES AND COACH TRAINING

The ICF provides ethics, standards and the core competencies for coaches, but not methodologies. Coaching schools train students on methodologies. It can be helpful to use coaches who are aligned on a particular methodology for your external coaches. Additionally, consider these schools to train all of your internal coaches using the same methodology. They may even train your internal coaches by coming to you.

CHAPTER 10:

IMPLEMENTING COACHING SKILLS FOR LEADERS

When you implement coaching skills for the leaders in your organization, you'll be setting up a training workshop. The person doing the training should be a coach, and they should have experience specifically in training coaching skills; Otherwise, they won't understand the important nuances—for example, the difference between mentoring and coaching. Make sure they're truly training *coaching* skills, not some hybrid.

If your trainees are eventually going to become professional coaches themselves, be sure your coach and trainer is a coach from an accredited institution so that the training hours can be applied to their coaching requirements for certification. These workshops often only total eight hours of training; regarding accredited coach training towards a credential, that's only a blink—but it can certainly be a motivating start!

Most importantly, find a coach that has a good rapport with the organization. As with any coaching engagement, you want to find someone who fits your culture and personality.

THE WORKSHOP

As far as the actual training goes, make sure there's a mix of specific coaching behaviors, as well as a model that your trainees can reasonably replicate. The late Sir John Whitmore's GROW Model, found in *Coaching for Performance*, is the simplest and most effective model I've used in training leaders with coaching skills. I personally do a lot of work on building rapport with the client: techniques for that, body language, how to be more approachable, etc. Then I'll follow that up with some training in active listening skills: paraphrasing, adapting to and using the client's vocabulary—little things that will help the client do less work, but might be a lot trickier to master than you think.

I also always talk about powerful questioning. We talk about things like how the word "why" can make people defensive; they feel like they have to justify. I generally avoid that word, unless I'm trying to be deliberately provocative for a very specific reason. (A recommended resource for this is *Leading with Questions* by Michael J Marquardt.)

We also talk about direct communication: how to make the observation for the client that will endorse them and help them stand in the conclusions they have. Then, we talk about designing actions: what is it the client is determined to do? What might get in the way? When are they going to do it? We always want to set the goals as a conclusion of the conversation.

TGROW: A coaching model with analogies

Topic	find an area of work to focus on.	COUNTRY
Goal	define exactly *what* you want.	CITY
Reality	explore where you are today, and what is stopping you from going forward.	GPS
Options	work out what you *could* do, generate ideas from the conscious and sub-conscious mind.	ROUTES

MANAGERS VS. COACHES

There are some distinct differences between managers being trained with coaching skills versus an actual coach. The biggest one is that the manager has an agenda. As much as they might try to suspend their agenda, they always have something they want the employee to do; after all, they're the ones who already gave the employee their performance objectives. If the employee says "I don't want to do that," in a coaching session, that's a problem.

Another issue for managers is learning to give up advising. I teach a lot of new students at Coach U, and they struggle in their first class when they learn they can't advise anymore (when purely coaching); often, that's what they thought coaching was. That's why they came to coaching school in the first place—but that's just not going to work.

If they're blending coaching skills with another profession that *does* include advising, it can work beautifully when done correctly. For example, if a financial advisor can learn to ask some open-ended questions about financial goals, about what you intend to do with your money and when you plan to use it, your comfort level with risk, etc., that's the coach approach. That works wonderfully if they can also shift gears and say, "Now that I've created this awareness for you, and I know your goals, here's some things I would recommend."

It's all about clarifying your shift—"I was coaching, now I'm _____, okay?"

That shift is especially important for managers. They need to be able to put their coach hat on, then their manager hat, and be clear about which is which. They will often try to use coaching skills when it comes to performance management, but that's not going to be effective. With performance management, there is an agenda, and there's a directive, which immediately cancels coaching out.

Say, for example, an employee is repeatedly late. If a coach addresses the topic with the employee, they might ask things like, "What factors are affecting your timeliness? How do you think your coworkers perceive your tardiness?" Those questions are great for coaching, to create some awareness for the employee as a client. But if that's a manager addressing the employee? Well, the fact is their agenda is for you to start coming in on time, and there's going to be consequences if you don't. They're not as detached as a coach.

When I'm training managers in these skills, I ask them to use something visually directive to the client that clearly says, "I'm shifting. I'm now putting my manager hat on. I've gone through all this discovery process with you, but we need to talk about this." Just like the financial consultant; they start with the coaching, then make a clear shift: "As your financial consultant, with all the information that you've shared, I want to suggest this."

If you can get past these hurdles, training your leaders in coaching skills can be extremely powerful and provide a return on your investment. For example, if you train 30 managers and they all have 10 people, 300 people will be affected in the process. It would take a significant period of time to coach 300 people individually!

FOLLOW-UP & SUPERVISION

The two biggest mistakes that people make when they implement a coach training workshop is that they don't do a follow-up, or they don't provide supervision. Trainees *always* need follow-up; after they've been using coaching skills for a month (or a designated period of time), they're going to have questions, they're going to need adjustments.

It's essential that the coach trainer has an opportunity to observe the managers practicing their coaching skills—that's the only way they'll catch them advising or mentoring, and be able to help them adjust accordingly. Again, managers often think they're coaching when they're not.

A great way to make sure you implement supervision *and* follow up is to learn one skill at a time. Start with one workshop, focused on one skill, after which the group has a month to practice and learn before the trainer returns to watch them in action. Then another workshop for a new skill, in the same pattern; if you leave room for asking questions in-between workshops, you have a lot of potential for focused growth. That might mean the coach comes in every Friday for follow-up, or the employees could just keep track of their questions throughout the month.

The follow-up and supervision are what determine the success for this modality. Any good training, in any skillset, needs these; coaching is no exception.

CHAPTER 11:

IMPLEMENTING INTERNAL COACHING

Internal Coaching is the most complex of the modalities, and because it is a significant long-term investment, I've identified 10 implementation steps for program success that are unique to this modality.

Step 1: Desire Isn't Enough

Just wanting to implement a coaching program won't fuel your coaching; you won't see lasting success without a goal. There has to be a specific business need you're trying to solve with coaching. You don't have to figure it out right away, but somewhere in that process, whether it's when you first hire the consultant or when you decide upon expansion, you have to determine the problem you're going to solve or the vision you are aspiring to. Do you just want a resource for all of the employees? Why? To develop high-potential leaders? Increase engagement in a certain department? Onboard new employees? Unless you have enough funding to provide everyone in the company with coaching, you're going to have to narrow your focus.

In my organization, I was one coach supporting an employee-base of ten thousand. The solution that we came up with was the group coaching. This was innovative; some organizations still only use one-on-one coaching. Starting with a group can prove to be either the biggest challenge or the highest opportunity. With that group, you can establish a proof of concept to demonstrate why it might be worth it to expand.

Step 2: Identify the Sponsor & Other Key Roles

We talked about sponsors briefly already, but make sure you know what their role is, if any, outside of funding the program. What is their experience with coaching? If none, get them a coach and be sure there is a goal for their engagement.

Often, companies will start with an external coach that can act as a consultant for implementing an internal coaching program; they'll coach the leaders, as well as mentor the internal coaching team. If there is a qualified internal coach who will also act as the program/project manager, how will they be mentored and supervised in their coaching role?

If there will be a team of coaches, you can hire from the outside using an industry standard qualification such as a credential from the International Coach Federation (ICF). Or, consider choosing highly respected, highly emotionally-intelligent employees who have proven an interest and gift for coaching (not advising, counseling, training or mentoring). Send them to an Approved Coaching Training Hours (ACSTH) or Approved Coach Training Program (ACTP) (both of these designations are from ICF training programs), and enjoy the advantage that these employees have of peer respect and knowing the company culture.

If you're hiring a consultant from outside, you'll start by requesting a proposal from that consultant; you might even post a job description, where only coaches need apply. In the same way that you would validate their credentials as an external coach, do the same when hiring an internal coach. In addition to making sure that they can fulfill the job responsibilities and the job description, you're also checking if they're a good fit for the company culture. Do you want someone distinctly different, or right in line, with your current culture?

JCPenney hired one of the chief officers from Apple to come in and run the company, looking to add a diverse voice to their culture. He thought about things differently; unfortunately, in this case, it did not work out. He tried to make JCPenney into Apple. People buy Apple as a status symbol; they don't expect coupons or discounts. But the loyal JCPenney customer counts on coupons, promotions, and more consumer-friendly ideas.

Then again, bringing in a different voice could provide a lot of benefit to your department. It depends on the features that you're looking for the coach to provide. If this is the only coach, they're also going to play the part of program manager. They'll be doing the administrative tasks associated with the coaching program, including the measurement of the program, the reporting of the program, giving status updates to leadership—not just purely coaching.

Picking a consultant from inside the company can be an advantage since that person will already understand the company culture and hopefully have a tremendous amount of respect from their colleagues. Just make sure they have a natural inclination towards coaching. There's a self-assessment that Coach U puts out to help you determine if you'd make a good coach. Particular behaviors and personality traits make a coach effective. For instance, they tend to be a good listener. They're highly motivated by enabling other people's success. They can take their satisfaction from other people's achievements as opposed to their own—which is important because once you become a coach, you don't have any of your own achievements when coaching. Your achievements are your client's achievements.

Similarly, if you find someone that tends to be judgmental or aloof, they may not be a good candidate for coaching. When I'm teaching my new students about this, I warn them. Their whole life, they've been paid for the judgment that they bring to things. Is it right or wrong? Is it left or right? Is it black or white? Should we go this way or this way? Which is better? We do this a thousand times a day, and that's the value that most coaches brought to their previous profession. But as a coach, you can't judge, you can't advise, you can't direct.

Step 3: Coaching for The Leadership Team

After getting buy-in and high recommendations from the sponsor, extend coaching to his/her leadership team, so they too can be advocates/evangelists for the effort. Sometimes people intuitively know coaching is a good thing, and they want to provide it like a benefit similar to medical coverage. But if your organization hasn't achieved this level of buy-in yet, the leadership team will be key for the support of this program.

Step 4: Seek Buy-In from the Leaders

After all of the leaders have had a chance to experience the benefits of coaching, and are seeing both personal and business results due to the coaching intervention, seek buy-in for the next step. Remember, there's a number of ways to evaluate the program and ROI is not the only way to do it. Sometimes, it's just return-on-expectation (ROE). Just like any scientific experiment, you create a hypothesis: "If we run this intervention called coaching, we will observe this kind of change in the environment."

Gaining sponsorship for establishing an internal coaching program can happen in several ways. Some organizations require data that shows a clear return on investment while others find anecdotal evidence of the impact of coaching sufficient. EY's in-house executive coaching practice started due to shifts in the business landscape that required leaders to transition and perform at the highest levels as quickly as possible. Sponsorship to invest in internal coaches for EY made sense from both an economic and strategic perspective

Dawn Pons, EY's Americas Director of Executive Coaching and Career Transitions, shared that every newly promoted partner receives an executive coach for the first 12-18 months in their role. It's offered as one of the perks of being promoted as well as to accelerate the success and impact of these leaders. EY has discovered that when their leaders receive coaching during defining moments in their career, they become better—faster. The clarity gained through coaching results in leaders with strengthened confidence, enhanced skills that maximize business results, and greater levels of professional and personal satisfaction.

Step 5: Train the Leaders in Key Coaching Skills

Once your leaders have been coached, and have a significant investment in this program, then implement a coaching skills training workshop for them. This guarantees that the leaders understand what the coaching process is. If management doesn't understand the process, they're going to confuse coaching with a touchy-feely good benefit—a nice thing to do, as opposed to a real business advantage which actually gives an ROI.

Step 6: Determine a Target for Your Pilot

Determine who within the business will most benefit from this program, keeping in mind the business problem you are trying to solve. Some goals may include: improving employee engagement, onboarding new or new to job employees; adjusting to a change management; developing leadership skills or improving employee -retention. Each of these goals has a specific audience you need to focus on.

Depending on the organization, it's usually useful to try and find the 'high-potential' employees. The high-potential is regularly defined as exceptionally skilled and deeply invested; the organization could move them to higher levels or to new geographies. The high-potentials are where we want to concentrate our investment because these are the future leaders of the company; they might be the leaders in their own domain today. We want to grow that capacity or scope of their leadership.

Typically, this is part of a company campaign. They've identified thirty people, and they want to provide them with some specific leadership training on the new level that they're being exposed to. In addition, they'll assign these trainees a particular project, and they'll assign you a coach.

Although this is a great application, it usually can only address a small number of people. Others, who are not given these opportunities are readily disengaged. They too, want the opportunities to grow. If they were given the opportunities, and that's where the group coaching sessions can be helpful—anyone who is self-motivated enough can attend. This is the self-help crowd: They're willing to go to the workshops, read the books, and do the seminars because they are eager to develop and learn. Honestly, those are my favorite clients to coach because they're so intrinsically motivated and curious.

Anyone who's new to the company is also a key target market. I can't tell you how many times I've had a new employee come to the work site and no one has assigned them a cubicle, or they don't have a computer ready for them. What are they supposed to do? They can't set up anything. They don't have a place to sit. Talk about not feeling welcome.

If on day one you can tell those new hires, "This is the training you're going through. After you complete this training, you have these many sessions with a coach, and you're free to ask them anything you want in those sessions. It's all confidential. It's not required, but we encourage you to go to at least two sessions before you make a decision about it." Those companies are tremendously successful in making sure that people start off on the right foot and ultimately stick around longer.

FOCUS: NEW MANAGERS

Brand new managers are often in desperate need of coaching. Sadly, too often the manager has been promoted, and they need to go to manager training, but because of budget cuts, they've canceled all of the manager training for the quarter. It could be a whole year before they go to manager training. But they need someone to help them establish good practices in that first year: how to hold effective staff meetings; how to do a performance review; delivering difficult conversations.

> "In a recent study, training alone improved leadership skills by 22%. When combined with Executive Coaching, improvement jumps to 77%."
>
> —FORTUNE

I'm always amazed when I get someone who's a new to director role because this is the first time they've had their own admin assistant, and they have no idea how to utilize them. What's the most effective way to put them to work? Traditionally, they'll say "I hate doing my travel. I want them to do my travel." Or "I want them to manage my calendar." You can say that, but if you fail to hold a discussion with your admin about the ground rules for managing your calendar, you're going to create more frustration than satisfaction. The effective managers have rules like "Accept any meeting that has to do with a customer right off the bat," or, "If it's an internal meeting, find out why I have to be there, and if I can send someone else."

The most effective execs, no matter where they are in the world traveling, they have a brief chat or live video conversation with their admins, coordinating about what's coming down the docket and what the admin should be ready for. The exceptionally effective executives have their admins run their administrative details, so they may just concentrate on the strategic work. That's why it's an executive admin position. The executive assistants, frankly, tend to have the most power in the company.

An internal coach is a good choice for 'new manager' clients because they know the culture of the company. In general, if they are providing good coaching and they're asking strong open-ended questions, they're revealing to the client what they already know, from their previous experiences, versus what they don't know, and who they need to find to answer those questions. This acclimation process of performing the new role, combined with the goals the new manager has set for the engagement, ensures a smoother transition for the new manager through the coaching partnership.

Step 7: Establish a Baseline for the Key Performance Indicators

IN CHAPTER 8 we've covered the Measuring the program...

Establishing a baseline means improvement can be attributed to the coaching intervention. In chapter eight, we referred to all of the possible measurement methods ranging in effort and formality. The only two requirements are choosing the measures and determining your baseline. The Key Performance Indicators (KPIs), of course, will depend entirely on your goals for the business and the target market you've chosen. These are in relation to the entire coaching program's success.

The individual client's KPIs will differ. One question to help your client prioritize is, "Do I want to make my best even better, or do I want to make my worst tolerable?"

I'm a big fan of making best better because it helps the leader stand out and makes the company stronger. That's playing to their strengths. The goal is to amplify strengths and manage weaknesses. When evaluating a client's strengths, how does the strength help them achieve their goals? How can we leverage the processes and habits and routines that make them effective and replicate them for other areas where they are not as successful?

MY PERSONAL SOAPBOX: THE HOMOGENIZED WORKFORCE

My audiences have heard me say this numerous times, but it bears repeating. Too many organizations in the yearly evaluation process identify employees 'opportunities' and make it a part of their development plan. As the employees strive to close the gap in their 'opportunity area', they neglect to continue to hone the strength that keeps them on the cutting-edge and an all-star in that area for the company. As a result, the entire organization becomes mediocre in all things—a homogenized workforce rather than a team of diverse strengths all-stars. An excellent resource to identify and celebrate a team's diverse strengths and apply them appropriately is the Gallup's StrengthsFinder Assessment. (see resources). Conducting the StrengthsFinder assessment with coaching clients and creating an action plan to utilize those strengths is one of the best investments a company can make.

Step 8: Establish Standard Operating Procedures

Develop a shared coaching agreement, for all the coaches, that includes standards for mentor coaching, feedback sessions, and a place to discuss common observations while maintaining confidentiality.

Every organization has this for their regular procedures. Coaching has some of those same guidelines, and every coaching engagement has to have a coaching agreement with agreed-upon procedures, including whether we're going to use the Kirkpatrick + Phillips model, or some other method, to collect the baseline for all of the clients and report accordingly.

This agreement also acts as the contract for the engagement, so it wouldn't do a company any good to have twenty coaches with twenty different agreements, or for a coach to have twenty different agreements for twenty different clients. The standard coaching agreement is an essential tool to help the coaches stay organized and the program to stay cohesive.

Often, if you're the program manager of a coaching program, you basically want to know your roster of coaches and their certification status, how many hours they coached. The organization may have standards: i.e. to coach managers, you need at least 100 hours and have your ACC; for execs, 500 hours and your PCC. *(ACC & PCC refer to different levels of certification for individual coaches bestowed by the ICF)* Those sorts of guidelines can be helpful as part of the shared operating procedures, so everyone's on the same page.

Also, within the coaching agreement is a reporting tool that tracks the collective hours that were coached. It's easiest to have the coaches do the reporting as to how much they coach each month and the levels of the people they coached. That way, collectively, the program manager and the consultant can report back to the company and say "We delivered 100 hours." The agreement makes that kind of synergy possible.

Step 9: Create a Marketing Presentation

For the coach, part of their standard operating procedures is what I call the dog-and-pony show. That's the presentation, the slide show, the pitch about what coaching is or isn't, and how you get started. Here's where you explain coaching and how it differs from other helping professions, taking great care to present it as a privilege, separate and distinct from 'corrective action' and other similar manager duties. During that little show, they'll probably pass out an intake packet, which the coaching agreement is usually part of. This might also include a questionnaire that helps the coach get to know the client more quickly. It might include a brief bio on the coach, so the client feels more comfortable with them.

All of the talent broker organizations have something like this to promote coaching, and if the internals want to keep justifying their position, they need it, too. It's easy for internals to think they don't have to promote this; that if they build it, people will come. Unfortunately, that's just not true. They have to be in front of their audience. They have to promote their accomplishments; they have to make their people aware of how valuable they are. All of the marketing tasks that external coaches have to do to keep their business profitable and have enough clients, the internals have to do, too. If you coach executives for a year and the year ends, no one's going to sign up for year two if you don't promote your program! Then, when the company needs to do a budget cut, guess who an easy target is?

THE MARKETING PRESENTATION

The internal coach must promote and market the internal coaching program just as an external coach would need to market their business. Once results have been collected, those results should be incorporated in the presentation. The following is a recommended outline of items to include in your presentation.

- What is coaching?
- Coaching vs. Mentoring
- The Benefits of Coaching (including research)
- Why it works
- Benefits for the company
- How to Get Started
- Next Steps
- How the Coaching Program fits with the Company's plans or Objectives
- Initial results/Established track record

Step 10: Measure Progress and Promote the Results

Once you have your measured results, decide if expanding your audience might be appropriate. Consider whether you need to make any adjustments to your practices or your target markets. Compare your current program to the other modalities and the cost per intervention, as well as intangibles such as attitude and cultural change.

Sometimes measuring can be difficult, because of the

confidentiality issue. Something I get asked a lot is: is coaching really confidential? I want to address this now because it's important that everyone understands: *yes*, in the coaching code of ethics is a requirement for firm-client confidentiality. Coaches can't even name their clients unless the client's given them permission to do so. The content of all their sessions is likewise completely confidential. Even if a manager has been directive about what the goals of the coaching engagement should be, and they're expecting progress reports, they can't expect to get a direct update from the coach. The coach isn't at liberty to say anything, even if they made the arrangement ahead of time. They can schedule an update with the coachee, but the coach can't lead the discussion.

I know managers who try to weasel around this all the time. They try to say "Well, I just want an idea. How do you think it's going?" I have to be careful to ensure that I'm not revealing something that I shouldn't. Even stuff like, "How is it going?" might be an indication to a coach that this is a performance management issue.

I feel very strongly that coaching is a privilege. When we talk about coaching, we're talking about clients that are creative, resourceful, and whole. We're not trying to fix something that's broken, even if the company thinks something's wrong. Sometimes, if it's an enlightened company, we talk about why this role was different than their previous roles, and what made them successful in their previous roles that might not be applicable here. Do we need to find a different role or do we need to just accept that they're not good at this particular behavior? There was no way they could anticipate that.

The perfect example of this is when organizations have teams of engineers, and they want to promote the best engineer on the team to be the manager. Well, the skill sets for an engineer versus a manager are different. It's an awful thing to do to the engineer even if they want a promotion. They might not be very equipped to be a manager or be a leader.

Collectively, all the coaches can have a generic conversation about the trends and themes they're observing in their coaching sessions. For example, everybody is griping about the new leader or everybody is griping about some new policy that's been enacted. The coaches amongst themselves may have that conversation without including client names. Sometimes, in a challenging situation, a coach may take a specific example to their mentor coach, but that mentor is also bound by the same confidentiality. Most coaches will have that in their coaching agreement: "I report your name or, depending on your company's privacy policy, an alias for your name and the number of hours I coached you so that ICF knows that I've done these coaching hours. They might contact someone in case of an audit on my coaching hours. I might go to mentor coach to ask for advice and guidance." Your clients should know that because they signed that standard agreement ahead of time.

Every organization I know uses some kind of alias so that the client isn't particularly identified in terms of their before and after scores for coaching. I always report them at an amalgam level, meaning on average, the coaching participant from the management level improved ten points on this scale—I never report in terms of an isolated client. That confidentiality is key, and paying close attention to it is never more important than within the internal coaching program.

CONCLUSION

WHAT IS COACHING?

Coaching is a partnership between a coach and client to achieve the client's goals. The coach does not advise or mentor, but uses a proven methodology to establish a trusting relationship with effective communication. This method uses awareness to design meaningful actions. The coach is both a cheerleader and accountability partner to ensure the client achieves their created goals.

WHY IMPLEMENT A COACHING CULTURE?

True coaching culture outperforms all other forms of leadership by allowing the leader to lead, creating and utilizing an engaged workforce. A coaching culture works collaboratively, submitting ideas, and takes ownership for the results. Companies with a strong coaching culture outperform their peers and have higher rates of engagement which translates to productivity, profitability, and retention.

WHAT ARE MY OPTIONS TO DO SO?
- External coaches
- Coaching skills for leaders
- Internal coaching

Or any combination of the above; the more modalities employed, the stronger the culture.

HOW DO I IMPLEMENT A COACHING CULTURE?

Begin with your leaders receiving coaching. The experience of coaching will outweigh any testimonials or research. Once the leaders understand coaching, you can jump to any of the modalities that your organization can fund. The investment will pay for itself and then some. Depending on your key performance measures, your ROE and ROI will vary.

As you finish here, don't forget about a few key ideas.

COACHING CAN BE USED ALMOST ANYWHERE

MANAGEMENT OF CHANGE

Whether it's acquisition, a merger, a new strategy, a new leader, or a new job, coaching can help people make sense of what's going on around them. It can create some clarity for your team: What was, what now is, and do they have any influence? Do they have any control?

One of the exercises that I do with my clients in the management of change is this: make a list on the left-hand side of a page of how everything was, and then on the right-hand side, what is *now*. Left, old manager; right, new manager. That sort of thing. Then, for the stuff that they're not sure about, they can explore. Some things they have control over, and some they don't. We do a separate exercise that deals with that, but just having someone to partner with through the change is valuable.

The biggest changes are usually when someone is transitioning into a new job, or transitioning under new management. Coaching can create the clarity of, "I know my old manager did it this way, but I'm not confident about how the new manager is going to do it." It's hard to ask that question without that awareness; it's difficult to be prepared if you don't explore what might cause stress.

WORK-LIFE BALANCE

Coaching may address implementing work-life balance; helping people set some boundaries about how many hours they're going to put in, what kind of projects they're going to work on, what their comfort level is with travel, and more. It can be about gearing up for a promotion, being proactive enough to ask the manager for assignments that will help better prepare them for that next step, developing a career plan—anything along the way.

CAREER COACHING

Sometimes there's a question of the job fit. Is this the right position for me? One of the observations that I've made over the years is that a lot of high-achievers have a habit of not saying no, which means they're eager to learn and develop—but sometimes they find themselves off their career path because they've taken whatever job they're offered. Coaching can help them take the time to analyze and say, "Am I happy with this, or do I want to go back to the direction where I was headed in the first place?"

STRESS MANAGEMENT

Sometimes, it can be difficult to recognize that you *are* off that pre-planned path, or that you need some support in the form of coaching. One common indicator is an actual physical ailment; stress can wreak havoc on your body, and often your body knows what you need more than you do. I've seen clients who take excessive sick leave, who get migraines, or who can't accomplish the same amount of work they used to. If your energy level has declined, or you notice your performance is slipping, do a check-in. A coach can help you look at that more clearly.

As an executive, keep an eye on these symptoms for your employees. Has there been a drop in productivity or confidence in your workforce? Is there a lot of stressed-out water-cooler talk? If one of your team is enlightened enough to speak up and say, "Hey. We've got a problem here. We've got to do something about it," make sure you take that seriously. Strong leaders have what I call some 'reverse mentoring' relationships; they have people lower down in the organization that they use as their ear to the ground. However, you do it, make sure you don't miss the signs when something's going on.

START-UP COACHING

Coaching is helpful in the conception phase of your business—the time you're forecasting, you're doing business strategy, you're establishing your vision, mission, or purpose. With all of those exercises within your new teams, a coach can help facilitate and bring in fresh perspectives, asking forward-thinking questions like, "If we were at *this* point, how would day-to-day look differently in this office?" In corporate, we often call it the green field:

we're starting from scratch. Everything's a clean slate, and a coach conversation can create even more opportunities.

CREATING STABILITY

This is a space especially for preventative coaching. One of my former leaders once said, "I really like to make changes when things are going well," because then, you can isolate the impact of the change versus trying to fix things that are already broken. This coaching early-on, this preventative coaching, is about creating that stability, especially with employee engagement. If you're proactively using coaching to keep challenging employees in a good way—they're working on their goals, they're moving forward—that will set a beautiful precedent.

DECISION-MAKING

Once, one of my colleagues was coaching someone as they tried to decide whether he wanted to leave the company and follow his calling. Initially, my opinion was: "I work for this company. I'm not going to coach you to go find another job." It didn't seem appropriate. In hindsight, with that particular example, it turned out to be a good thing; they were able to replace him with someone who was engaged, and he stopped distracting his colleagues with his dilemma.

NOT COUNSELING OR MENTORING

The only topic that would not be appropriate for a coach would be something that is clearly a mental-health issue. We would absolutely need to refer them to a mental-health provider or psychologist. Similarly, if the client is clearly more interested in developing subject-matter expertise, we might refer them to a mentor instead of a coach.

As long as a coach is truly coaching and staying in the coaching domain, they can always make great changes.

REMEMBER: COACHING OUTPERFORMS OTHER LEADERSHIP STYLES

A coaching leadership style, or a coaching culture, is going to outperform other methodologies of leadership because it's easier for the manager. It's less work. It engages the entire workforce and encourages them to submit their innovations and ideas to the manager—who, again, isn't doing that work for them. People felt more motivated and attached to an outcome when it's their own idea, so managers are freed up to lead and manage.

When I think of the manager's job, it's to catch and distribute the work. It's the actual employee's job to *do* the work. By freeing managers up to lead, they're able to do a better job looking out on the horizon and looking sideways, while the employees look down and focus internally.

When people are out of trust mode, they literally become addicted to being right. That's what we call the *Tell, Sell, Yell* syndrome. They're going to tell you, then they're going to try and convince you and compel you, and then if you're still not doing it, they're just going to yell at you. Coaching can build trust, as well as get us out of that place of distrust, back to where employees are intrinsically motivated to do the work and managers are leading from a place of creativity, positivity, growth, and trust.

When the manager is free, and employees are engaged, the organization is more curious; they are open to new and innovative ideas or different ways of doing things. One of my former colleagues, Danny Dalrymple, the Canadian Services Director of a Fortune 50 company, managed a team of experts who were all excellent in their roles, but were growing stagnant; they'd been doing the same thing for too long. He took half the team and shuffled them around into each other's roles. It was the musical chairs of job functions; he switched it up, and then they started applying their previous perspectives to these new roles. It broadened the ideas that could be applied, created new uses, new applications and even new markets for existing products! The previous stewards hadn't thought of any of those applications—they were too focused on doing it right and being accurate, as opposed to being curious.

YOUR NEXT STEPS

Now that you know you want a coaching culture, it's time to engage a coach that can start a dialog with you. How can you create a plan that will be ideal for your company together? My own company offers extensive coaching, as well as consulting on how to implement your own coaching program using any or all three of the coaching modalities (External Coaching, Internal Coaching, and Leaders with Coaching Skills). If you're curious (and remember, you should always be curious!), contact us. Let's see if we're a good fit. If not, I know many other coaches and their specialties, and I would be happy to refer you to another practitioner. You have nothing to lose by engaging a coach for that first conversation, which is usually free. Engage, and share what your challenges are; then you'll get some initial ideas for what the opportunities are. Even if it's not in your budget right now, that first free conversation can give you a feel for the budget and effort required to reach your goal of building a coaching culture. Then you can put it into the forecast and business planning objectives for the next fiscal year.

Contact: Shawna Corden www.shawnacorden.com

GLOSSARY OF TERMS

Assessment: A method to determine scientifically-verifiable and statistically-significant findings. Often used in coaching relationships to determine personality types, leadership styles, strengths or other information helpful to the client's development.

ACSTH: Approved Coaching Specific Training Hours (ACSTH) program accreditation is intended for third-party training providers who are interested in having their training program accredited by the International Coach Federation (ICF). ACSTH-accredited programs are considered "al la carte" training programs, which may or may not offer start-to-finish coach training programs. A minimum of 30 student contact hours are required for ACSTH program accreditation.

ACTP: Accredited Coaching Training Program (ACTP) accreditation is intended for third-party training providers who are interested in having their training program accredited by the International Coach Federation (ICF). ACTP accredited programs are considered "all-inclusive" training programs, which offer start-to-finish coach training. A minimum of 125 student contact hours, Mentor coaching and a performance-evaluation process are required for ACTP approval.

Coaching Agreement: An agreement, sometimes referred to as a contract between the client and coach outlining expectations of the relationship for the engagement

May also refer to the focus and desired outcome of an individual coaching session.

Coaching Certification: Demonstration of proficiency in coaching—three levels awarded by the ICF

- ACC: Has completed 60 coach training hours and delivered at least 100 hours of coaching
- PCC: Has completed 125 coach training hours and delivered at least 500 hours of coaching
- MCC: Has completed 200 coach training hours and delivered at least 2,500 hours of coaching

Coaching Engagement: Refers to the entire duration of the time the coach and client work together.

Coaching Supervision: Coaching supervision focuses on the development of the coach's capacity through offering a richer and broader opportunity for support and development. ICF is committed to provide opportunities to coaches to consistently develop and grow professionally. Coaching supervision creates a safe environment for the coach to share their successes and failures in becoming masterful in the way they work with their clients.

Code of Ethics: ICF is committed to maintaining and promoting excellence in coaching. Therefore, ICF expects all members and credentialed coaches (coaches, coach mentors, coaching supervisors, coach trainers or students), to adhere to the elements and principles of ethical conduct: to be competent and integrate ICF Core Competencies effectively in their work.

Consultant: Subject-matter expert trained in a given field to provide a skill, or provide advice on processes or actions.

Counselor/Therapist: Trained experts in the field of counseling or mental health that provide advice.

External Coach: A coach working with a company or individual but not employed by the company.

Gallup's Q12: Gallup knows how organizations can create engaging workplaces. It starts with measuring & managing the 12 elements of employee engagement. They've seen these strategies work in countless companies across the world, no matter the industry or workforce. And they've created solutions for organizations of all sizes, to help them engage the people they lead.

Learn more about what they know about employee engagement, and how they can help you strengthen & engage your workplace at q12.gallup.com

HCI: At the Human Capital Institute (HCI), their work makes work better. HCI delivers live and virtual educational content to human resource teams, talent management leaders, and business executives around the world to help them plan, build, and develop the workforce of the future. They are a privately-held, entrepreneurial company, focused on innovations that help organizations get the maximum impact out of their most valuable asset: their people. Learn more at *www.hci.org*.

Internal Coach: A coach employed by the company they coach for.

The International Coach Federation (ICF): The governing body for professional coaches that accredits schools and certifies individual coaches.

Kirkpatrick: The Kirkpatrick Four-Level Training Evaluation Model helps trainers to measure the effectiveness of their training in an objective way. The model was originally created by Donald Kirkpatrick in 1959, and has since gone through several updates and revisions. It includes four levels: Reaction, Learning, Behavior, Results.

Kirkpatrick + Phillips: Adds a fifth dimension to the four levels of the Kirkpatrick, adding the calculation of Return on Investment (ROI).

Leaders with Coaching Skills: Individuals trained in coaching skills, regardless of title, practicing coaching with their peers or subordinates. Typically, have limited training hours, and are not professional coaches.

Performance Management: Performance management is a process by which managers and employees work together to plan, monitor and review an employee's work objectives and overall contribution to the organization.

Prism: In 2005, ICF Global adopted the Prism Award, a concept developed by ICF Toronto to recognize outstanding organizational coaching initiatives. Today, the International Prism Award honors businesses and organizations with coaching programs that fulfill rigorous professional standards, address key strategic goals, shape organizational culture, and yield discernible and measurable positive impacts.

Professional Mentor Coach (PMC): The ICF defines Mentor Coaching as providing professional assistance in achieving and demonstrating the levels of coaching competency demanded by the desired credential level sought by a coach-applicant (mentee). Furthermore, Mentor Coaching means an applicant (mentee) being coached on their coaching skills rather than coaching on practice building, life balance, or other topics unrelated to the development of an applicant's coaching skill.

Mentor: Subject-Matter Expert who provides advice to another individual with less experience or expertise than they have. May be a formal or informal relationship. Advice is usually not in exchange for money.

ICF CODE OF ETHICS

Preamble

ICF is committed to maintaining and promoting excellence in coaching. Therefore, ICF expects all members and credentialed coaches (coaches, coach mentors, coaching supervisors, coach trainers or students), to adhere to the elements and principles of ethical conduct: to be competent and integrate ICF Core Competencies effectively in their work.

In line with the ICF core values and ICF definition of coaching, the Code of Ethics is designed to provide appropriate guidelines, accountability and enforceable standards of conduct for all ICF Members and ICF Credential-holders, who commit to abiding by the following ICF Code of Ethics:

Part One: Definitions

Coaching: Coaching is partnering with clients in a thought-provoking and creative process that inspires them to maximize their personal and professional potential.

ICF Coach: An ICF coach agrees to practice the ICF Core Competencies and pledges accountability to the ICF Code of Ethics.

Professional Coaching Relationship: A professional coaching relationship exists when coaching includes an agreement (including contracts) that defines the responsibilities of each party.

Roles in the Coaching Relationship: In order to clarify roles in the coaching relationship, it is often necessary to distinguish between the client and the sponsor. In most cases, the client and sponsor are the same person and are therefore jointly referred to as the client. For purposes of identification, however, the ICF defines these roles as follows:

Client: The "Client/Coachee" is the person(s) being coached.

Sponsor: The "sponsor" is the entity (including its representatives) paying for and/or arranging for coaching services to be provided. In all cases, coaching engagement agreements should clearly establish the rights, roles and responsibilities for both the client and sponsor if the client and sponsor are different people.

Student: The "student" is someone enrolled in a coach training program or working with a coaching supervisor or coach mentor in order to learn the coaching process or enhance and develop their coaching skills.

Conflict of Interest: A situation in which a coach has a private or personal interest sufficient to appear to influence the objective of his or her official duties as a coach and a professional.

Part Two: The ICF Standards of Ethical Conduct
Section 1: Professional Conduct at Large

As a coach, I:

1) Conduct myself in accordance with the ICF Code of Ethics in all interactions, including coach training, coach mentoring and coach supervisory activities.

2) Commit to take the appropriate action with the coach, trainer, or coach mentor and/or will contact ICF to address any ethics violation or possible breach as soon

as I become aware, whether it involves me or others.

3) Communicate and create awareness in others, including organizations, employees, sponsors, coaches and others, who might need to be informed of the responsibilities established by this Code.

4) Refrain from unlawful discrimination in occupational activities, including age, race, gender orientation, ethnicity, sexual orientation, religion, national origin or disability.

5) Make verbal and written statements that are true and accurate about what I offer as a coach, the coaching profession or ICF.

6) Accurately identify my coaching qualifications, expertise, experience, training, certifications and ICF Credentials.

7) Recognize and honor the efforts and contributions of others and only claim ownership of my own material. I understand that violating this standard may leave me subject to legal remedy by a third-party.

8) Strive at all times to recognize my personal issues that may impair, conflict with or interfere with my coaching performance or my professional coaching relationships. I will promptly seek the relevant professional assistance and determine the action to be taken, including whether it is appropriate to suspend or terminate my coaching relationship(s) whenever the facts and circumstances necessitate.

9) Recognize that the Code of Ethics applies to my relationship with coaching clients, coachees, students, mentees and supervisees.

10) Conduct and report research with competence, honesty and within recognized scientific standards and applicable subject guidelines. My research will be carried

out with the necessary consent and approval of those involved, and with an approach that will protect participants from any potential harm. All research efforts will be performed in a manner that complies with all the applicable laws of the country in which the research is conducted.

11) Maintain, store and dispose of any records, including electronic files and communications, created during my coaching engagements in a manner that promotes confidentiality, security and privacy and complies with any applicable laws and agreements.

12) Use ICF Member contact information (email addresses, telephone numbers, and so on) only in the manner and to the extent authorized by the ICF.

Section 2: Conflicts of Interest

As a coach, I:

13) Seek to be conscious of any conflict or potential conflict of interest, openly disclose any such conflict and offer to remove myself when a conflict arises.

14) Clarify roles for internal coaches, set boundaries, and review with stakeholders, conflicts of interest that may emerge between coaching and other role functions.

15) Disclose to my client and the sponsor(s) all anticipated compensation from third-parties that I may receive for referrals of clients or pay to receive clients.

16) Honor an equitable coach/client relationship, regardless of the form of compensation.

Section 3: Professional Conduct with Clients

As a coach, I:

17) Ethically speak what I know to be true to clients, prospective clients or sponsors about the potential value of the coaching process or of me as a coach.

18) Carefully explain and strive to ensure that, prior to or at the initial meeting, my coaching client and sponsor(s) understand the nature of coaching, the nature and limits of confidentiality, financial arrangements, and any other terms of the coaching agreement.

19) Have a clear coaching service agreement with my clients and sponsor(s) before beginning the coaching relationship and honor this agreement. The agreement shall include the roles, responsibilities and rights of all parties involved.

20) Hold responsibility for being aware of and setting clear, appropriate and culturally sensitive boundaries that govern interactions, physical or otherwise, I may have with my clients or sponsor(s).

21) Avoid any sexual or romantic relationship with current clients or sponsor(s) or students, mentees or supervisees. Further, I will be alert to the possibility of any potential sexual intimacy among the parties including my support staff and/or assistants and will take the appropriate action to address the issue or cancel the engagement in order to provide a safe environment overall.

22) Respect the client's right to terminate the coaching relationship at any point during the process, subject to the provisions of the agreement. I shall remain alert to indications that there is a shift in the value received from the coaching relationship.

23) Encourage the client or sponsor to make a change

if I believe the client or sponsor would be better served by another coach or by another resource and suggest my client seek the services of other professionals when deemed necessary or appropriate.

Section 4: Confidentiality/Privacy

As a coach, I:

24) Maintain the strictest levels of confidentiality with all client and sponsor information unless release is required by law.

25) Have a clear agreement about how coaching information will be exchanged among coach, client and sponsor.

26) Have a clear agreement when acting as a coach, coach mentor, coaching supervisor or trainer, with both client and sponsor, student, mentee, or supervisee about the conditions under which confidentiality may not be maintained (e.g., illegal activity, pursuant to valid court order or subpoena; imminent or likely risk of danger to self or to others; etc.) and make sure both client and sponsor, student, mentee, or supervisee voluntarily and knowingly agree in writing to that limit of confidentiality. Where I reasonably believe that because one of the above circumstances is applicable, I may need to inform appropriate authorities.

27) Require all those who work with me in support of my clients to adhere to the ICF Code of Ethics, Number 26, Section 4, Confidentiality and Privacy Standards, and any other sections of the Code of Ethics that might be applicable.

Section 5: Continuing Development

As a coach, I:

28) Commit to the need for continued and ongoing development of my professional skills.

Part Three: The ICF Pledge of Ethics

As an ICF coach, I acknowledge and agree to honor my ethical and legal obligations to my coaching clients and sponsors, colleagues, and to the public at large. I pledge to comply with the ICF Code of Ethics and to practice these standards with those whom I coach, teach, mentor or supervise.

If I breach this Pledge of Ethics or any part of the ICF Code of Ethics, I agree that the ICF in its sole discretion may hold me accountable for so doing. I further agree that my accountability to the ICF for any breach may include sanctions, such as loss of my ICF Membership and/or my ICF Credentials.

For more information on the Ethical Conduct Review Process including links to file a complaint, please click *here*.

Adopted by the ICF Global Board of Directors June 2015.

RESOURCES

An Educated Approach: Nurturing a Coaching Culture at Isikkent Schools, (ICF article), 2013 Case Study, available at the ICF website: https://www.coachfederation.org/ or directly here: https://coachfederation.org/files/FileDownloads/IsikkentCaseStudy.pdf

Being Coached: Group and Team Coaching from the Inside, Ann V. Deaton & Holly Williams, 2014, MAGUS Group

Building a Coaching Culture, White paper 2014, International Coach Federation (ICF) & Human Capital Institute (HCI), available here: https://coachfederation.org/coachingculture

Building an Internal Coaching Pilot, Coaching World, March 2017, available here: https://coachfederation.org/blog/index.php/8167/

Coaching Basics, Lisa Haneberg, 2006, Association for Talent Development

Coaching for Performance: GROWing Human Potential and Purpose—The Principles and Practice of Coaching

and Leadership, 4th Edition, John Whitmore, 2009, Nicholas Brealey

Conversational Intelligence, Judith E. Glaser, 2013, Bibliomotion, Inc.

Creating a Coaching Culture for Better Talent - Organizational Snapshot: GlaxoSmithKline, ICF PRISM award, available at the ICF website: https://www.coachfederation.org/ or directly here: https://coachfederation.org/files/FileDownloads/CaseStudy_GSK.pdf

Drive: The Surprising Truth About What Motivates Us, Daniel H. Pink, 2009, Riverhead Books

Expectation vs. Agreement, Steve Chandler, http://www.stevechandler.com/audio.html

Management Time: Who's Got the Monkey?, William Oncken Jr. & Donald L Wass, Harvard Business Review, Nov-Dec 1999, available here: https://hbr.org/1999/11/management-time-whos-got-the-monkey

ICF Member Develops "Coachability" Survey, Coaching World, July 2009, available here: https://www.coachfederation.org/files/includes/docs/july09.pdf

Kirkpatrick Model, available here: http://www.kirkpatrickpartners.com/Our-Philosophy/The-Kirkpatrick-Model

Measuring the Success of Coaching: A Step-by-Step Guide for Measuring Impact and Calculating ROI, Patricia Pulliam

Phillips, Jack J. Phillips, Lisa Ann Edwards, 2012, Association for Talent Development

Now What? 90 days to a New Life Direction, Laura Berman Fortgang, 2004, TarcherPerigee

Peer Feedback Video by Marshall Goldsmith, available at www.youtube.com/watch?v=qK0FXR6UAFO

Retreats That Work, Liteman, Liteman, and Campbell, 2006, Pfeiffer

StrengthsFinder 2.0, Tom Rath, 2007, Gallup Press

The 5 Second Rule: Transform your Life, Work, and Confidence with Everyday Courage, Mel Robbins, 2017, Savio Republic

The 7 Habits of Highly Effective People, Steven Covey, 1989, Free Press

The Coaching Conundrum Report, 2016, Blessingwhite, available from: http://blessingwhite.com/research-report/2016/05/09/the-coaching-conundrum-report-2016/

The Coaching Habit: Say Less, Ask More & Change the Way You Lead Forever, Michael Bungay Stanier, 2016, Box of Crayons Press

The First 90 Days, Updated and Expanded: Proven Strategies for Getting Up to Speed Faster and Smarter, Michael Watkins, 2013, Harvard Business Review Press

The ONE Thing: The Surprisingly Simple Truth Behind Extraordinary Results, Gary Keller, 2013, Bard Press

The Values Americans Live By, L. Robert Kohls, available from: https://careercenter.lehigh.edu/sites/careercenter.lehigh.edu/files/AmericanValues.pdf

Three Minutes to Midnight: What's the Point of Coaching, Neil Scotton & Alister Scott, Coaching at Work, Jan 2016 available here: http://www.coaching-at-work.com/2016/01/05/three-minutes-to-midnight-whats-the-point-of-coaching/

Transitions: Making Sense of Life's Changes, Revised 25th Anniversary Edition, William Bridges, 2014, Da Capo Press

What Can Coaches Do for You?, Diane Coutu & Carol Kauffman, Harvard Business Review, Jan 2009, available here: https://hbr.org/2009/01/what-can-coaches-do-for-you

Made in the USA
Columbia, SC
17 January 2019